Tales

of the

Himalayas

ISBN: 1-4033-1029-7 (e-book)
ISBN: 1-4033-1030-0 (Paperback)

Library of Congress Control Number: 2002103488

This book is printed on acid free paper.

Printed in the United States of America
Bloomington, IN

1stBooks - rev. 7/2/02

Tales

of the

The Himalayas

Letters from WWII Airmen
who flew the Hump
and from other
Veterans of the CBI

Compiled and edited by

Dr. Carl Frey Constein

DEDICATION

To the memory and honor
of those who served

in the mountains of China,

in the jungles of Burma,

in the valleys and plains of India—

and never returned

TABLE OF CONTENTS

Also by Carl Frey Constein

Born to Fly the Hump
A Memoir

A WWII pilot recalls his 96
round-trip C-46 flights across the Himalayas

Orchestra Left, Row T
A Novel

A Hunp pilot finds it difficult
to readjust to civilian life

Sadie's Place
A Novel

A school superintendent's struggles
in the decade of the Sizzling Sixties

PREFACE

MEETING IN OTTAWA three months after Pearl Harbor, President Franklin D. Roosevelt, Prime Minister Winston Churchill, and the Allied Command determined that China should be kept in the war as a base for the ultimate invasion of Japan. In spite of the valor of the Flying Tigers, Japanese planes cut the Burma Road. The only alternative was to fly supplies from India to China across the jungles of north Burma and the Himalayas of China. Thus was born the "Hump," history's first airlift.

A C-46 pilot, I was sent to India in October 1944 to join thousands of airmen flying treacherous 500-mile and longer Hump routes made even more dangerous by the world's worst weather. I recalled my 96 round-trips in a WWII memoir, *Born to Fly the Hump.* Of the many Hump/China-Burma-India veterans and their families who read my book, hundreds have written to me. Some readers sent succinct "short takes" or sincere notes of appreciation. A few sent photographs. Pilots and crews wrote of bailouts, mammoth storms, engine failures, of bombing runs and airdrops and carrying troops behind enemy lines in Burma. Other CBI veterans whose assignments were on the ground told of rugged conditions in the high mountains of China, the dense jungles of Burma, the monsoons and heat of India.

I was fascinated by the letters; they vividly demonstrate how diverse and comprehensive the CBI theater was. As I read Tom Brokaw's compilation of WWII letters *An Album of Memories,* it struck me that I too should share mine with readers. *Tales of the Himalayas* is the result. In a small way, the letters may compensate for the neglect of the Hump/CBI by most historians.

Compiling the letters has been more than fascinating, it has been enriching. In my golden years, my circle of friends and acquaintances has burgeoned. I thank each letter writer. I wish I could meet them all in person.

By Tuesday, September 11, 2001, I was well into the manuscript. After a week of profound incredulity, sorrow, and anxiety, I returned to the book with a renewed purpose to tell our special WWII story. As we were sixty years earlier, perhaps in the current conflict our generation can again be a symbol for love of country, for devotion to duty.

Carl Frey Constein

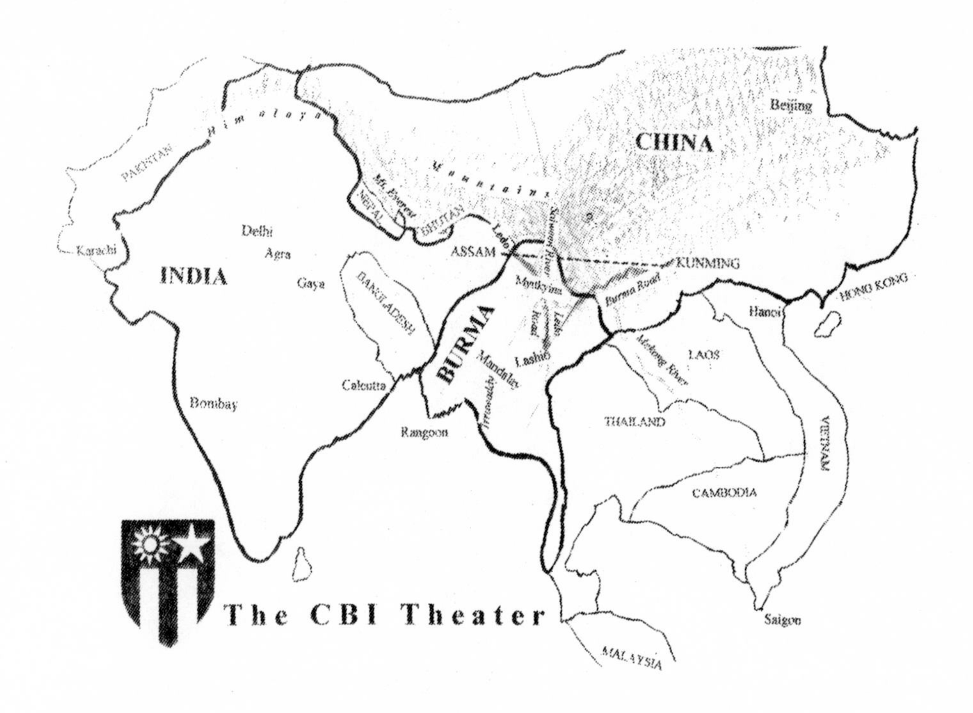

The CBI Theater
CHINA
Beijing
INDIA
PAKISTAN
Himalaya Mountains
Mt. Everest
NEPAL
BHUTAN
Delhi
Agra
Gaya
Karachi
Bombay
Calcutta
BANGLADESH
ASSAM
Ledo
Salween River
KUNMING
Burma Road
Myitkyina
Ledo Road
BURMA
Mandalay
Lashio
Irrawaddy
Rangoon
HONG KONG
Hanoi
LAOS
Mekong River
THAILAND
VIETNAM
CAMBODIA
Saigon
MALAYSIA

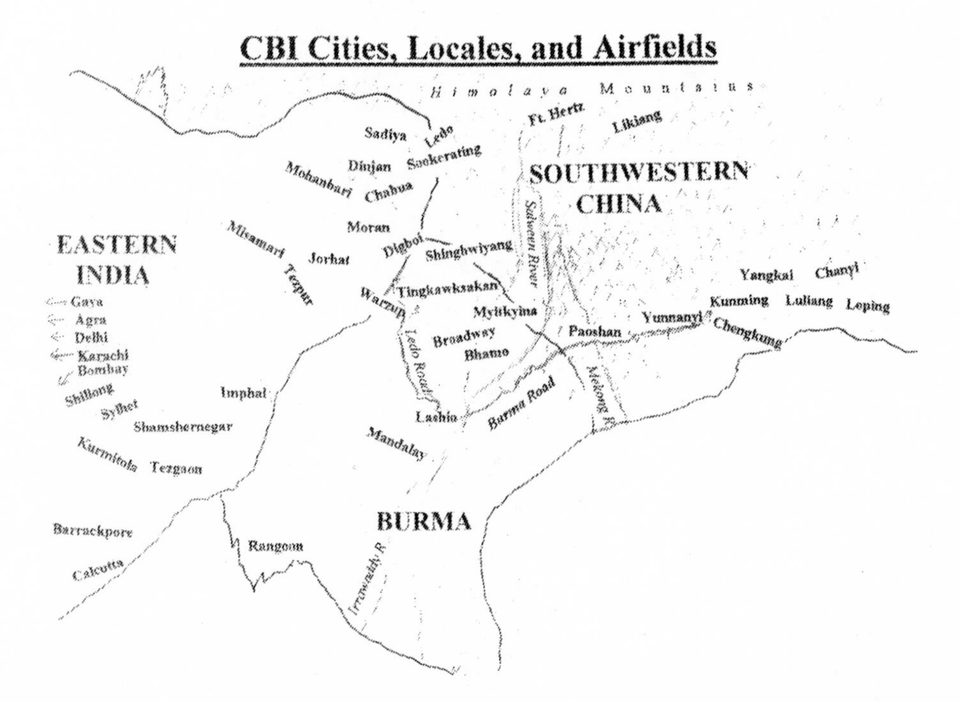

CBI Cities, Locales, and Airfields
Himalaya Mountains
Sadiya
Ledo
Dinjan
Sookerating
Mohanbari
Chabua
Ft. Hertz
Likiang
SOUTHWESTERN CHINA
Moran
EASTERN INDIA
Misamari
Jorhat
Digboi
Shinghwiyang
Tezpur
Salween River
Tingkawksakan
Warazup
Myitkyina
Yangkai
Chanyi
Kunming
Luliang
Leping
Gaya
Agra
Delhi
Karachi
Bombay
Yunnanyi
Chengkung
Paoshan
Broadway
Bhamo
Ledo Road
Shillong
Sylhet
Imphal
Shamshernegar
Lashio
Burma Road
Mekong R.
Mandalay
Kurmitola
Tezgaon
BURMA
Barrackpore
Rangoon
Calcutta
Irrawaddy R.

PART 1

LETTERS AND NOTES GALORE

EIGHTY PERCENT of the Americans who served in the CBI in World War II were attached to the Army Air Corps, as it was then designated. My own assignment, although dangerous, was a bit of a bore at times—pile into a C-46 on the strip at Chabua, fly three hours to China, mostly to Kunming, remain on the base while Ole Dumbo is unloaded, fly four hours back to India. Three days later, repeat the operation. Many air crews had more variety in their assignments—including Air Transport Command crews based in Burma and China, Troop Carrier and Air Commando squadrons, and crews of the 10th, 14th, and 20th Air Forces.

Our planes were flown by experienced Service Pilots, Air Corps ferry or bomber/fighter pilots sent in from the States or from other overseas assignments, or by spanking new Aviation Cadet graduates like me, still wet behind the ears. Many radio operators and crew chiefs had extensive experience in other theaters before coming to the CBI.

On the ground were other US groups—General Vinegar Joe Stilwell and his staff advising the Chinese army; Brigadier General Frank Merrill and his Marauders behind enemy lines in Burma; troops and engineers building the Ledo Road; and communications, support, medical, and service groups of all kinds, some in ghastly jungle outposts. Totally, 120 commands, base units, and organizations carried out their assignments in the CBI. For all of us, the awesome Himalayas were a constant reminder of where we were—and how far we were from home.

Tales of the Himalayas is a book you will enjoy best by reading only a handful of letters at one sitting. As the English essayist Francis Bacon said about books, some letters are to be… “tasted, others to be swallowed, and some few to be chewed and digested.”

Hendersen Harbor, NY

Dear Carl,

Your classic story of the Hump calls me back! We were in a holding stack together somewhere, I wager. It seems strange to have been so close to other fields in the valley (Assam Province, eastern

India) but to have visited so few of them. I lost one basha-mate at Tezpur; never learned the site of his demise. I still correspond with the pilot who helped deliver a new C-87 to the pool of Hump planes. Lt. Col. Roland E. Speckman was a career pilot in the AF in B-47s and B-52s; he found relief in being cross-qualified in choppers and rescue in Vietnam.

Thanks for making your story available to our families. As for Brokaw's The Greatest Generation, *I'm adding your book as a last chapter.*

Sincerely,
Fred Stone

Beavercreek, OH

Dear Dr. Constein

I flew the Hump from December of 1943 to June of 1944. I had 300 hours on the Hump and a lot of valley time.

When I left Misamari with 15 other crews, we went up to Teheran and then to Russia in bomb support missions. In July I was transferred to Tunis as C-47 pilot. On January 1, 1945, I had the worst and scariest flight of my life in a Mediterranean snow storm.

We were scheduled to take passengers from Algiers to Tunis that day. When the air became very rough, we climbed to 10,000 feet to escape the turbulence. I went back to the cabin to check my sorry lot of French-speaking passengers—unwashed bodies, babies, passengers sick from the turbulence. When I returned to the cabin and saw we were at 14,000 feet, I nearly jumped out of my skin. "What are you trying to do?" I asked the copilot, "set an altitude record for old planes?"

Turbulence increased. Ice formed on the windshield. Airspeed fluctuated between 100 mph and 180 mph. We were tossed up and down, at times peering straight down at the ocean then suddenly straight up at the sky. It was really violent; I nearly bought the farm.

I have inquired whether this convoluted Mediterranean storm might have wound up on the Hump on January 6, giving so many guys a hard time. (►I was one of those guys.) *If you have any input on this, I'd like to hear it.*

Congratulations on your many Hump flights. I'm sure you did some for me, and I appreciate it.

Respectfully,
Joseph H. Steinbicker

►Colonel Steinbicker's query is intriguing. I read that the probable cause of the Hump's monster storm of January 6-7 was a merging of a low front over the Himalayas, a high from the Bay of Bengal, and another low from Siberia. Dr. Otha C. Spencer, author of *Flying the Weather,* might be able to answer the question. Steinbicker gives a more detained account of the North African storm in his book *How Come I'm Still Here?*

(►Please note: Wherever I felt a brief annotation would add to the reader's understanding or enjoyment, I added it, preceded by a pointer symbol. Readers may also find helpful the Glossary of terms and abbreviations. It is located near the back of the book.)

Carmel, CA

Dear Carl:

As former Chief Pilot at Jorhat during the winter of 1944-45, I look forward very much to receiving a copy of your book. Congratulations on telling the story, which seems to have had a lasting effect on those of us who participated in the great adventure...and were blessed with getting out alive!

Sincerely,
Ralph H. Miner

Belleville, NJ

Dear Carl,

Like you, I graduated from Cadets on August 4, 1944. You received your wings at Waco, Texas; I got mine at Blytheville, Arkansas. I graduated as a Flight Officer. In a class numbering one hundred ninety-nine, 79 were appointed F/Os. I never found out why. There could not have been that many goof-offs.

After transition training in the C-47, I was sent as first officer to the 443rd group in Shingbwiyang, Burma. After Burma was secured, we moved to Dinjan, India, to continue our supply missions by flying C-46s over the Hump into China. I flew more than 50 such missions. Totally, I ended up with 124 missions, 504 combat hours, the Air Medal with two Oak Leaf clusters. Fifty-four years later, in 1999, I was awarded the DFC.

Steve Ambrose is writing a book about the war in the Pacific. I don't know whether he is reaching into the CBI, but for his information I sent him a five-page letter about our overlooked theater. I couldn't resist singing the praises of the C-47s I flew. As Troop Carrier pilot, I ferried troops into Burma and dropped essential supplies into remote areas behind enemy lines. No other cargo plane, I told him, could fly into jungle strips no longer than an aircraft carrier.

It's hard to believe what you and I and thousands of others did. So young, so innocent!

Regards,
Len Kriegman

►I was fortunate to receive a 2nd Lieutenant's commission., but I too was always puzzled by Flight Officer status. It was equivalent to the Army's Warrant Officer. It had to do with the number of commissions which were available, but, except for granting the F/O rank to the obvious goof-offs referred to by Len, I never learned the rationale for distributing them.

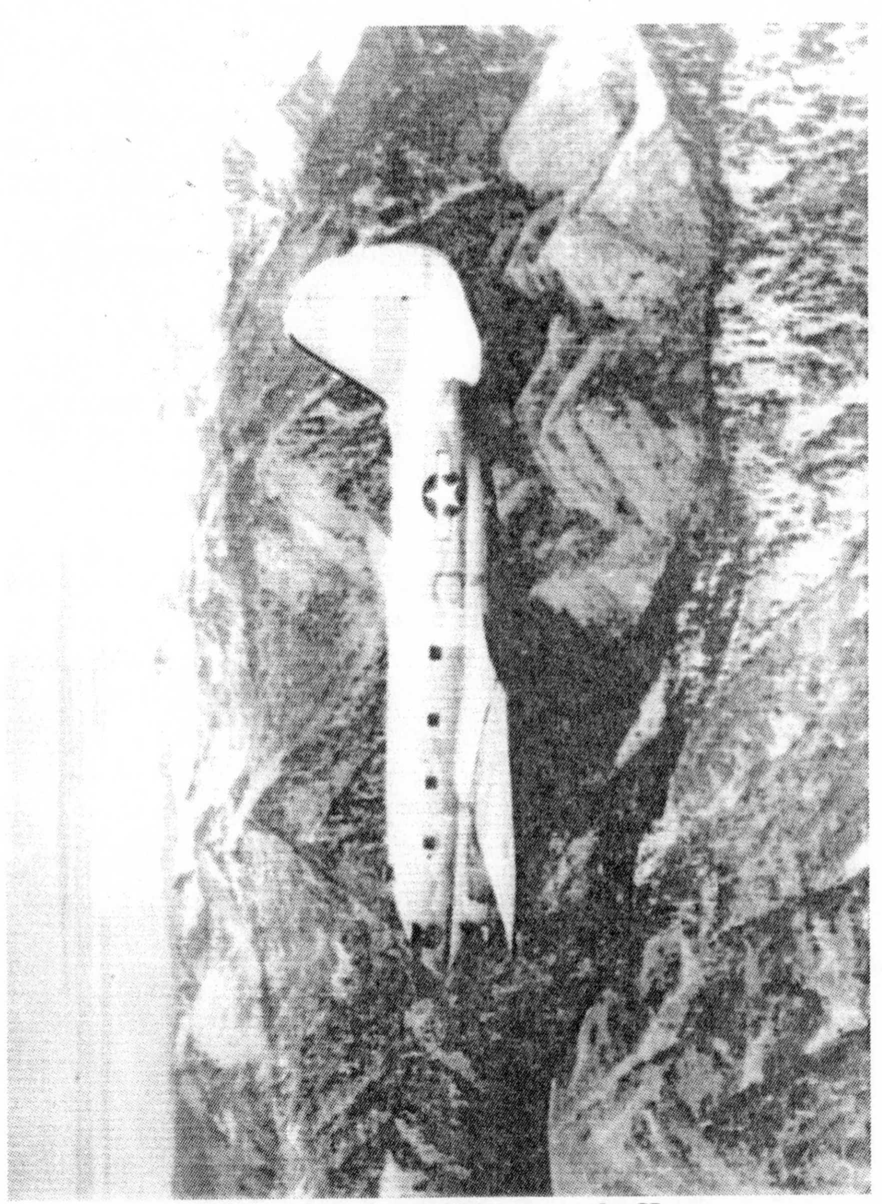

A C-46 returns from China over the Hump

Philadelphia, PA

Dear Dr. Constein,

You probably don't remember me, but I'm the big guy who bought your book at the Mid Atlantic Air Museum's WWII Weekend in Reading. You inscribed it in memory of my dad, who was a Timberwolf of the 104th Infantry Division.

Reading your book, I laughed out loud when you described how you as an MP were assigned to "guard" the coal piles of Philadelphia Electric's Grays Ferry Avenue Station. As a Philly cop, presently a sergeant assigned to court liaison, I have driven by the electric company for more than twenty-two years. I have most likely slept many times in the middle of the night near where you were assigned. Now I too ponder that question: who was guarding the coal piles before you arrived? I have also been assigned to Belmont Plateau many times for city affairs. Now when I drive by I will think of you and your fellow MPs of the 722nd Battalion, which, according to you, was the most chicken outfit in the whole US Army. In over two decades I too have worked for supervisors like your CO and drill sergeant. Now when I cut my toenails I will always wonder—is the right way straight across or rounded?

I am pleased to add your book to my extensive WWII collection. I hope to see you at the 12th WWII Weekend at the airport next June.

Sincerely,
Joel Belsky

Avon Park, FL

Dear Carl,

Just a quick note to thank you for writing your memoir. I identified completely with so much of it. I was a radio operator—21 round-trips west to east, then was transferred to the China side—Chengkung, Chanyi, and Kunming. My service was from June '44 to

October '45, a long time ago, but so many emotions surfaced. Some memories are good, some bad, some frightening.

It's good to realize there are still some left who shared the same experiences. It was a good thing too that we were young and thought we were destined to live through it all.

God bless!
George Corcoran

Bernville, PA

Dear Carl,

I enjoyed reading your book Born to Fly the Hump. *I always maintained there were not enough words in the English language to describe flying through a thunderstorm. You found them!*

I was fortunate during my tour of duty in the CBI.

First: I flew a brand-new C-54 from Nashville, TN, to India. I did not have to deadhead. We departed on March 26, 1945, and, after 16 days and 73 flight hours via South America, Ascension Island, Aden, and Karachi, we arrived in Kurmitola on April 10.

Second: The C-54 was a great four-engine airplane, flight-tested in the USA—unlike your plane, the C-46, which was sent to the Hump without thorough testing. I don't have to tell you how many problems that lack of testing caused.

Third: My base at Kurmitola had twenty-five C-54s and twenty-five C-109s (B-24 tankers). The base at Tezgaon needed first pilots and our base at Kurmitola needed copilots. My first scheduled flight was to be on a C-109, a plane many pilots feared, labeling it the "109 Boom!" Luckily for me, before that flight I was transferred as first pilot to Tezgaon, which had C-54s only, 50 of them. So all my time over the Hump was in the dependable DC-4, designated by the Army Air Corps the C-54.

Fourth: The C-54 carried a heavy load but could not fly high altitudes like the C-47, C-46, C-87, or C-109. (The C-87 and C-109 were cargo versions of the B-24 Liberator bomber.) Consequently, the

C-54 was assigned a lower, more southerly Hump route. Trips were a bit longer—five hours on the eastern route—but safer.

Fifth: *By the time I arrived in India, the Japanese had been pushed so far south in Burma that I saw only three Japanese planes in flight, two Betty bombers and one transport. The danger for all Hump pilots, on almost all flights, was the world's worst flying weather. I flew in it for eight months, logging 615 hours. I was awarded two Air Medals.*

Several weeks before the end of the war I had two flights to Liuchow, China. On the first I had to land on the dirt taxiway because the Japanese had mined the runway. They were still fighting in the hills around the field—so close, in fact, that I could hear the gunfire! On my second trip there I again had to land on the dirt taxiway, this time because a B-25 landing before me had his landing gear collapse. Liuchow was the dividing line between our forces and the Japanese. All the land east of Liuchow to the Pacific and north to Russia was in Japanese hands. It was necessary to get our troops to Shanghai to accept the surrender and take control of the city. General MacArthur could not spare any troops so the CBI had to do it.

Carl, are you familiar with the Cannon Project? Not many Americans are, even fellows like you who had a lot of Hump time. The project was named for Colonel Andy Cannon, who ran it. It was one of the most spectacular and important operations in Air Corps history. It has received little attention because when it took place we were all happily celebrating the end of the war. Since the two atom bombs brought on the Japanese surrender so abruptly, the Japanese still occupied a large portion of eastern China, with no Allied troops anywhere near them. The closest troops of any size were the Chinese 94th Army stationed at Liuchow. They had to be moved from Liuchow to Shanghai. There were no improved roads, railroads, or canals by which to move the troops overland. The US Navy said they could do the job, but only after the mines had been cleared. That was a three-month job. After that, the Navy would require another three months to move so large a contingent. The only alternative—as a few years earlier when the Burma Road was blockaded and the Hump itself began—was to do the job by air. The Hump's last CO, General William H. Tunner, writes about the Cannon Project in his book Over the Hump. (*Tunner was later CO of the Berlin Airlift.)*

"Suppose, for example, that our planes were based in Los Angeles, that the 30,000 Chinese were to be flown from Atlanta to Boston—and that there was not a drop of gasoline nor one item of equipment or aircraft parts east of the Rockies. That would just about size up the situation.

"Our solution to the problem may sound a little bizarre at first, but there was no other. Each plane, before leaving its base in Bengal, would have its gas tanks filled to the maximum, and additional drums of gas to the maximum allowable weight would be loaded as cargo. The big C-54 would then fly over the Hump to Liuchow, where the drums would be unloaded. The airplane's tanks would be replenished with gasoline from these drums for the round trip to Shanghai. On its return to Liuchow, the plane's tanks would be filled again from the reservoir it had itself brought over as cabin cargo, and would return to its base in Bengal to perform the whole procedure over again. The total round trip would amount to 4,615 miles, all to fly one planeload of 80 soldiers and their equipment 1,100 miles to Shanghai."

On the first day of that project, I was the first plane to taxi out at Liuchow to take off for Shanghai. An Infantry captain pulled up in a jeep and called up to my window, "Regardless of when you take off, do not land in Shanghai before ship number so and so." (I have no notes on the these details.) In five hours we were over Shanghai. The other plane had not called in, so I had to fly around Shanghai for 20 minutes until he arrived. After he landed, I put down and taxied in behind him. I then understood the mysterious order from the captain back in Liuchow: I had one Chinese general aboard. He had one Chinese general and two American generals!

The mission was completed ahead of schedule. In 19 days we moved 26,237 troops of the Chinese 94th Army 1,100 miles to Shanghai. While we were doing this we also started "Project Hope," flying home-sick GIs from China to India to start their trip home. Taking advantage of the 200 C-54s stationed on the Hump, averaging 1,000 passengers a day, by the middle of October we had flown 20,000 men from China to India.

Carl, you may recall our conversation some time ago when I told you I flew more hours per month after the war ended than during the war. Checking my Form 5 Flying Time Record, I note: July - 92 hours; August - 98 hours; September - 121 hours!

During my tour in the CBI I ran into five pilots from home, two in China, three in India. I met Tom Masano at Chengkung and Ed Angstadt at Chanyi. You may recall that painted on the Flight Operations building in Chanyi was the elevation (one mile above sea level) and a word of commendation to the Hump crews: "Congratulations! You made it again!" At his base in Calcutta I met Brooks S. McElroy, and as they were passing through Tezgaon on their way home, I met Dave Bickel and Bill Spatz.

When the time came for me to go home, I was again fortunate. I flew a C-54 from Tezgaon to West Palm Beach, Florida, via Karachi, Cairo, the Azore Islands, and Bermuda. We left India on December 2, 1945, and arrived in the states on December 6—sixty-six hours flight time.

So, Carl, except for the weather, I had a good CBI tour.

John H. Schach

Amsterdam, Netherlands

Dr. Carl Frey Constein

May I introduce myself. My name is Francois Luxembourg, copilot 747 cargo plane. A month ago I was visiting the Chiang Kai-shek memorial in Taipei. I learned a lot about the work the pilots had delivered to their freedom.

My captain and good friend Gerald Van Pelt flew the DC-3 and DC-4. He read your book Born to Fly the Hump, *and I in this way would purchase seven copies.*

My father, Frans Luxembourg, has been flying since he was 12 years old on all kinds of singles and twins commercially and as instructor. The funny thing is the DC-3 was the biggest plane he used to fly for I believe five years. As for me, they promised me I am going for training in May for captain of 767.

I am very proud to be able to give my good friends and colleagues a signed copy of the real deal.

Do you still fly?
Hope you are in good health and Best Wishes in 2001.

Sincerely,
Francois Luxembourg

Alexandria, VA

Dear Dr. Constein,

My name is Miki Louis and I am a registered nurse in the med/surg ICU at INOVA Fairfax Hospital in Falls Church. A couple years ago I had the privilege of taking care of Lt. Col. George Wenrich, USAF Ret after by-pass surgery. During that time he and I bonded, and he and his wonderful wife are affectionately known to me as Aunt Joyce and Uncle George.

I recently had dinner with them, and Uncle George told me he had run into a college classmate. That would be you. As I had inquired earlier about his WWII days as an Army Air Corps pilot, he lent me an autographed copy of your memoir, Born to Fly the Hump. *He told me that except for one very unpleasant flight, the experiences you related were very close to his own.*

I have just finished your "Solo" chapter. Let me quickly confess that I know very little about the China-Burma-India theater of war or World War Two itself. Now at the ripe old age of 34, I recall my high school history classes going only as far as the Great Depression. But I do know that were it not for people like you and Uncle George, I'd probably be writing this letter in German. Because of people like you two, and without ever having to be personally involved in a war, I get to enjoy freedom, which I hold very dear. I cannot say thank you enough. I feel a responsibility to you and to those who follow me to preserve that freedom for which you and millions of others sacrificed so much.

I'd like to return Uncle George's copy of your book directly and have my own copy. My check is enclosed.

Please know that your service to our country is greatly appreciated.

Regards,
Miki Louis, R.N.

▶I believe Miki was speaking for a great many young Americans who are going out of their way to say thanks to veterans. Until two years ago, no one ever said thanks to me. Although WWII veterans are not looking for thanks, certainly not for praise, it is extremely gratifying that Americans are realizing that freedom is not free. George and I appreciate Miki's kind words.

Munhall, PA

Dear Dr. Constein:

I was the last personnel sergeant to serve the 253rd QM Remount Squadron up to the date of its deactivation. The squadron was activated on March 5, 1943, at Ft. Reno, Oklahoma. After it reached full strength, the squadron was sent to assignment in India. We arrived in Karachi and a short time later were shipped to Calcutta. A week later we began our long, torturously slow train ride to Pandu in eastern India. The ride was dirty, foul-smelling, bug-infested. But how can I ever forget riding through the vast plains of India—drums beating, natives chanting, the air filled with the odor of burning cow dung. We finally made it to Pandu. From there we boarded a stern wheeler out of the Mark Twain era to cross the broad Brahmaputra River.

We arrived at out permanent station at Shillong in the Khasi Hills. Our first job there was to build a remount depot. In October of 1944 a troop of another squadron arrived with the first 30 horses. By December the census of animals at the depot had escalated to 1,600. Additional Indian and American remount forces joined us. By May of 1945 the census had skyrocketed to 3,600.

The horses and mules were shipped from the states and some from Australia. They were used in Burma, mainly by Merrill's Marauders and the 124th Cavalry Regiment known as Mars Task Force. The animals arrived in Calcutta and were then hauled by rail and tractor-trailers to our depot in Shillong. They were used in the dense jungle to transport artillery, ammunition, tents, food, medicine. Under enemy fire they evacuated wounded troops. We depended on them; we got to love them. We'd cling to their tails up the trails and through the streams. A few GIs are alive today because a mule stopped a bullet meant for them. Mike, Ragtail, Rajah, Charlie, Myrtle, Flop Ears and many others I never knew were mortally wounded in battle.

In December of 1945 the Foreign Liquidation Commission was charged with disposing of all horses, mules, and equipment of the Remount Depot. Just like a GI, every animal had its own 201 file. They were run through chutes and the Army serial number tattooed behind the left ear was checked against the record. We maintained 3x5 cards detailing date of birth and acquisition, type, color, medical shots, disabilities, station, use (pack, riding, wagon, training, etc.) and final date of disposition. One shipment of animals was sent to Eastern European countries under Lend-Lease. Another shipment went to China and the Philippines.

On one very gloomy January day, 125 horses and 75 mules which were incurably diseased were rounded up and led to a trench 20 feet deep, 20 feet wide, 200 feet long. An Army veterinary officer fired a 45-caliber slug into the skull between the eyes. Those of us who watched had heavy hearts and lumps in our throats. A sentimentalist, I asked the officer-of-the-day for permission to fire a farewell volley in salute to those courageous animals, a proud contingent of CBI history.

We could not head stateside until all the animals were disposed of. The remaining horses and mules were sold to local villagers, and the sales were going mighty slowly. Then one day three ragged, dirty natives marched in and surprised us by plopping down rupees from five carpet-bagger suitcases. They bought the remaining 950 horses, 73 mules and all surplus equipment! We were on our way home!

After all these years I can clearly remember this Remount, the last in the CBI, possibly the last in the US Army.

Edward A. Rock, Sr.

►Rock's account of the Last Remount has been used by Boyd Sinclair in his series *Confusion Beyond Imagination,* volume 10, and by Melvin Bradley in *The Missouri Mule, His Origin and Times,* volume 2. It was also included in the Ex-CBI Roundup.

Aurora, CO

Hi Carl,

I arrived in Chabua in January of 1944 as a line officer in maintenance and left in December of 1945 after being director of aircraft maintenance for the base. Needless to say, I had continuous contact with all flight personnel during that period and would not believe we never met in some fashion. Unfortunately, at 78 my detail memory is no longer clear for events that took place over 55 years ago.

Sincerely,
John Cross

►I was always amazed at how aircraft maintenance did their job and kept our C-46s flying. At the India end of a twelve thousand mile parts-supply line, working outdoors, plagued by monsoon rains (100 inches a month in June, July, and August) and oppressive heat in other months—the job seemed impossible. I may have conferred with John one day when I couldn't get my plane off the ground on takeoff because it veered sharply right. After three attempts, I cancelled the flight.

Overland Park, KS

Dr. Contein,

My husband was also a pilot who flew the Hump. Our children, who are in their 40s, have no interest in this at this time, but hopefully one day they will and will then appreciate the sacrifice young men made in WWII.

Mary F. Stewart

P.S. My husband has a D.D.S. degree and has written his memoirs.

▶ Ms. Stewart is not alone in observing the apathy of young people about WWII. But in presentations to historical societies and other groups, and especially in CBI/Hump briefings I give at the Mid Atlantic Air Museum in Reading, PA, I have discerned a definite change. For the first time ever, people have thanked me for serving! I am fortunate too that my daughter has a genuine interest in the history of the WWII generation.

Kileen, TX

Dear Dr. Constein,

Two weeks after I graduated from a trade school in San Antonio, I received my "greetings" from the draft board. What I really hoped to do in the service was fly, but I lacked the educational requirement to apply for Aviation Cadets. Instead of waiting to be called (probably into the Army) I volunteered for the Army Air Corps to try to find a place in aircraft mechanics. I filled out the forms and was about to undergo the physical exam when the recruiting officer decided it was too late in the day. I went back to my aunt's house where I stayed while I was in San Antonio, went ice skating, fell and injured my knee, and spent four months recuperating. What a fortunate accident that turned out to be.

While I was healing, the Army Air Corps, in desperate need of pilots, dropped the requirement of two years of college for Cadet training, substituting instead an equivalent mental exam. My formal education had ended in tenth grade, but I kept up with my reading and decided to give it a shot. I passed, took preflight training at Lackland Field, then was sent to Primary flight school in Coleman, Texas.

The townspeople were very kind to servicemen. I soon learned that if you stood around long enough after church, someone would invite you home for Sunday dinner. I turned down two invitations one Sunday, hoping for an invitation instead from Mrs. Billings, whose daughter, Margaret, was really cute. Mrs. Billings came through.

After I received my wings and commission, I was assigned to the Air Transport Command and sent to Alpena, Michigan, the first of many fields, before I received the order I eagerly awaited—Miami, Florida.

Meanwhile, Margaret and I were corresponding. Between assignments I was able to visit her in Coleman, and yes, she promised to wait for me.

After a week or so, orders were cut for me to leave for India. The C-47 on which I was a passenger took the southern route over South America, then on to lonely Ascension Island. The line was, "If you miss Ascension, my wife gets a pension." Finally we arrived at our destination, Agra, India, home of the Taj Mahal. My assignment was to fly supplies to bases around India.

One day a call went out for pilots to go to Dinjan, India, on detached service with the 2nd Troop Carrier Command, which had lost half its planes and a third of its pilots to Japanese Zeros. The only three volunteers were Texans—Arnold Dube, William Wheeles, and me. Our mission was to fly supplies from Dinjan to an airstrip in Shingbwyang, Burma, in support of Allied troops pushing into the jungle. The strip was so short that every time I made a safe takeoff I felt it was a major victory. On our missions to drop supplies to Merrill's Marauders, we flew our C-47s at treetop level—and did a lot of praying. On one desperate mission we were to supply ammunition to troops that had been ambushed by the enemy. We couldn't locate them because of cloud cover. Flying low, we finally spotted a hole in the clouds, spied the troops, and dropped the full load. We pulled up into a steep climb, entered the clouds and prayed. A few minutes later we flew into bright sunshine and thanked the Lord we had not crashed into a mountain.

Back at Agra I started flying the airline again. Dube, Wheeles, and I applied for R&R in Srinagar, Kashmir. The town is built around a shallow lake. What a beautiful site. We rented a houseboat. We took a few excursions by water taxi. In town I bought a beautiful jewelry box made from a single piece of walnut. It still sits on our bedroom dresser. Srinigar was great not only because of its beauty but also because it helped me get over my resentment at being pulled off the action with the 2nd troop Carrier Squadron and returned to the boring flying out of Agra.

Weather on this "valley" flying was deceptively turbulent at times. The air is simply too dry to form clouds. One night I was flying at 8,000 feet in smooth air when suddenly the plane went into a severe shudder from front to tail. The instruments went crazy. I was going down so fast the altimeter needle couldn't gage it. I pulled up the nose and gave the throttles full power. It had no effect. I glanced out the window and saw the ground coming up fast. Suddenly I felt a bump. Just as quickly as we had gone into the danger we came out of it. I looked out and saw we were about 500 feet off the desert floor. I was still shaking when I got out of the plane an hour later in Karachi.

Time was fleeting. I became concerned that I might finish my tour of duty without ever getting to see China. Dube, Wheeles, and I put in for reassignment to one of the Assam "Hump" bases. Three weeks later we deadheaded to our new home, Misamari. A new adventure in flying was about to begin, this one in the larger, more powerful C-46.

The first ridge of mountains we crossed on our 500-mile trip to bases in China was the Naga Hills. Then came the Hukawang Valley. It was often covered by a layer of clouds that reached the mountain passes. It reminded me of a giant bowl of whipped cream that spilled over the rim and down the sides of the bowl. It was a lovely site. After that on our route we crossed the mile-deep canyon of the Salween River, so deep that sunlight didn't hit the canyon floor until noon, and the sun set at 3:00 p.m. Next was the canyon of the mighty Mekong River.

By the time I started flying the Hump, Japanese fighter planes were busy in Burma, no longer a threat to us. Our enemy was the weather, especially turbulence and ice storms. I still love to fly, but to this day, the thought of flying through an ice storm sends a chill up my spine.

I needed fifty hours to be rotated home. The magic day finally came and I landed my C-46 safely in Misamari. I had thought it might be a time of throwing my cap into the air, a big Texas cowboy yell on my lips. But none of that: I simply felt numb. I was required to remain in the CBI for two more months, mainly testing-flying planes after they had major overhauls.

Finally, in Karachi, my name was called to board an ATC passenger plane bound for home. The morning after we landed in Miami I slowly woke up, looked around and saw nice wallpaper on the walls, the bright sun shining through the windows, the palm trees outside the window gently blowing in the breeze. For a moment my groggy mind couldn't figure it out. Where was I? Slowly it all came flooding back. My tour in the CBI was complete. The incredible journey was over. I was back in the States!

Best regards,
Monroe Withers

►Withers wrote a short book entitled *A Texan in the CBI.* Withers' style is straightforward and appealing. In addition to the book, he sent along two poignant poems he wrote, one memorializing a friend who was killed in France in WWII, the other a tribute to his wife, who passed away in 1999, "...after 54 wonderful years of marriage. About a year later, from somewhere down in a deep pit I wrote these words...

Lend me Your Hope

Do you have a smile you could spare?
There's a hole in my heart it might fill.
I think I lost mine on that long, lonely road
That I traveled when Margaret was ill.

Do you have a warm hug you don't need?
Sometimes at night it gets cold.
And I look towards her chair
But there's nobody there
And the walls look faded and old.

Do you have some joy you can share?
I lost mine while mowing the lawn.
It was safe in my pocket
Up close to my heart
And the next time I looked it was gone.

Lend me your hope for the future.
I'll hold it a little while
And I'll dream of a time
When the future was mine
Then I'll give it back with a smile.

The Poppies of Flanders Fields

They tell of a time in the long, long ago
In a fair and gentle land
Where the grass was green and the sky was blue
And the beach was of pure white sand.
And the clouds grew pink as they hung in the west
In the twilight's afterglow.
And the beautiful poppies
That covered the land
Were as white as the driven snow.

Then the war drums sounded over Flanders Fields
And the soldiers tramped over the land.
The sword and the spear
Lashed out in hate
And the blood flowed free in the sand.
Then the war rolled on and the people came home
So dazed they could hardly think.
And they say that the poppies
That bloomed in the spring
Were edged in a delicate pink.

For a while there was peace in this gentle place.
Then World War One struck the land
And the blood that flowed over Flanders Fields
Was more than some could stand.
They fought in the trenches, they fought in the fields
And many of them wondered why.
And they say that the poppies
That bloomed in the spring
Were as pink as the evening sky.

When I was a lad I had a close friend
And we played many games in those days.
Then World War Two overshadowed the land

And we each went our separate ways.
I fought the war in a distant field
In mountains covered with snow
While he fought the war
On Flanders Fields
Where the beautiful poppies grow.

As he watched the guns belch out their fire
And watched the airplanes soar,
He wondered why men would die
In the insanity of war.

Why does a man leave his loving friends?
Why leave a home and a bed?
And they say that the poppies
That bloomed in the spring
Were tinged with streaks of red.

When I came home I rushed to his home;
His mother was at the door.
She reached out and gave me a loving hug
As she had often done before.
Then I looked o'er her shoulder and saw my friend
In a picture that hung in the room.
And beneath the picture was a Purple Heart
And some poppies that opened in bloom.

Will men ever learn to live in peace?
Will they ever trust God up above?
Will my friend's sacrifice be all in vain?
Will they ever trade hate for love?

He will never hold a loving wife
Or watch his children grow.
For he sleeps tonight
Beneath Flanders Fields
Where the blood-red poppies grow.

Sinking Spring, PA

Dear Carl,

A year before you came to your India base at Chabua, I settled in at Sookerating just to the east. I was attached to the 1st Troop Carrier Squadron as C-47 copilot/navigator. Our mission was to drop supplies from treetop level to Chinese troops in Burma. It was good duty, made even better because three other officers and I lived off base in a cottage on a British plantation of prized Assam tea.

Victor Parker was the manager. He and his wife, Bunte, invited us over to the "big house" several times a week for dinner or for high tea on the shaded lawn. Always gracious, Bunte allowed us American cousins to keep our beer cold in her refrigerator. Victor became a much-appreciated father figure to us. The Parkers left India and returned to England to enroll their daughter, Miki, in boarding school. Much later, after the war, I received a letter from Bunte. Engrossed in finishing my law degree, I never found time to answer.

Commemorations surrounding the 50th anniversary of WWII piqued a renewed interest in my CBI service and my English hosts. I had stayed in the Air Force Reserve, eventually retiring as a colonel. I used that connection to try to track down the Parkers. No luck. I wrote to the tea company, to the town council of the town where they had lived, to Scotland Yard, to a BBC radio program "Where Are They Now?" I got nowhere.

A break came four years ago when I met up with one of our quartet of officers who shared that tea cottage so many years ago. He had a letter from Bunte which referred to the convent school Miki had attended. I wrote to the school. The letter was forwarded to the former principal, Sister Maura Clune, who is now serving in an Elderhostel retreat house in Ireland. Luckily, she had kept in contact with Miki and led me to her.

On my 80th birthday two years ago, my wife, Edwina, and I visited Sister Clune at her Elderhostel. We visited Miki and her husband, Lawrence Bishop, in Chichester, England, twice. They visited us here in 2000, and we are looking forward to their second visit this October 2002.

My tour of 18 months in the CBI theater was a great experience, and my memories of that time are priceless.

Best regards,
Bud Speidel

Delray Beach, FL

Hello Carl,

I believe I remember you from Chabua. I was bunked in the last basha out in the tea patches and so were you. Did your family come from the Shenandoah Valley? Chambersburg? Did you leave me a dictionary when you were rotated home? It was the most extensive one I had ever seen outside a library, and I was most pleased to accept it. Thanks again.

Sincerely,
Mat Wiland

►I grew up not in Chambersburg but in another small town in eastern Pennsylvania named Fleetwood. Antique car aficionados know about the famous Fleetwood Auto Body Company. I can't recall the incident you speak of, but it sounds like me. I certainly would have had a dictionary in the basha.

Campbell, TX

Dear Carl:

While a senior at East Texas State Teachers College I took Civil Pilot Training, got a private license and enlisted in the Air Corps for pilot training. When war was declared, I was called up immediately and began my training in the class of 42-H in January 1942. After receiving my wings and commission, I was assigned as instructor in B-25s at Columbia, SC.

Students can come up with seventeen different ways to kill you on training flights! So I volunteered as one of four crews to fly experimental hurricane recon from Goosebay, Labrador, to Greenland with *the 10th Weather Squadron. Later we flew the same missions in the South Atlantic and Caribbean.*

Weather pilots had a spooky assignment—piloting a plane in severe weather, on instruments, hurtling at 200 mph through a visual nothingness. Instrument flying was the most threatening part on any flight, yet most pilots, especially at the beginning of the war, received precious little instruction in actual weather situations. But actual experience has always been the best teacher.

My first heavy weather flying was in the back of a C-46 en route to Presque Island, Maine. The weather was near freezing, low clouds, snow and rain. I was sure we would all die. I looked around the huge plane and saw, scrawled in chalk on the aluminum bulkhead of the pilot's compartment the ubiquitous mantra "Kilroy was here!"

After the hurricane season ended, we were sent to the CBI to fly weather recon missions up and down the Bay of Bengal and over the fearsome Himalayan Hump. Experience had proved that synoptic weather flights were more accurate and valuable in forecasting weather than were reconnaissance flights on the routes themselves. From Gushkara and Barrackpore, India, we flew mainly over the Bay of Bengal, a volatile breeding ground for great storms and fronts that moved into India, Burma, and on into the Himalayas and the Hump itself. Official monsoon rainfalls were between 425 and 500 inches of rain a year, with one hundred inches each month in June, July, and August.

Inaccuracies in forecasting raised the ire of Col. Thomas Hardin, hard-driving CO of the Hump operation. He decreed that from that time on "There is no more weather over the Hump." Interpretation? Crews could no longer cancel flights or turn back because of weather. Weathermen were affectionately known as "balloon blowers." The historian of the 10th Weather Squadron wrote, "Weather was a small tadpole in a big pond of croaking frogs."

In June of 1945 we were assigned to Chabua, India, on temporary duty, flying cargo to China as though we were in the ATC. I ended up with 21 round-trips. Carl, I respect your 96 missions.

When the war ended, we were assigned to close the weather stations in China. As we headed for our new base in Shanghai, we made one last flight over the Himalayas, tipping our wings to

Kunming as we flew over that busy eastern hub of the Hump. From November through March 1946 we covered the whole of ancient, enigmatic China. We were too young and too eager to get home to appreciate the priceless adventure we were having. Those last missions were filled with foreboding. To die in combat is a tragedy, but to die after the war cleaning up the mess of battle, marking time until you can leave for home—that too is a story of great anguish.

Thanks, Carl, for jogging my memory—of St. Elmo's Fire, of ham and eggs on the Kunming flight line, of Billie's restaurant in Kunming, of Lake Tali, of flying into Myitkyina, of the plume of Mt. Everest.

Otha C. Spencer

▶Dr. Spencer is the author of two excellent books on the subject—*Flying the Weather,* published by The Country Studio, and *Flying the Hump,* published by Texas A&M University Press.

▶Raymond Hoffman of Newark, Delaware, wrote to me. He served in the CBI with the same weather squadron.

San Marcos, CA

Dear Mr. Constein,

My husband, Max, and his brother Bill both flew the Hump in B-24s. Bill said that reading your book was like walking in the past; things he had forgotten came back.

Max, who is now in an Alzheimer's home, responds so well to your book when I read it to him. He shakes his head and smiles. So for both of us, it has been wonderful.

You have done us all a wonderful thing to preserve the history you made. Thank you.

Sincerely,
Eileen M. Hargis

▶In a note on a Christmas card, Eileen informed me that her husband passed away. She gave permission to use the letter she had sent me earlier.

Reno, NV

Dear Carl,

I was from a large Norwegian family from Great Falls, Montana. After I graduated from high school in 1938, I was lucky to find a summer job on a wheat ranch for $2.00 a day plus room and board. In the fall I found a permanent job as a flour tester at General Mills. Then, after I received a Federal Grain Inspector license, I accepted a position as inspector for the Montana State Grain Laboratory. In that job I was deferred from military service in World War Two.

I asked to be released from that deferment and in October 1943 went to Butte to take the test for Air Corps Cadets. Both my brother John and I passed and at the end of January left by train for Los Angeles. After the rigors of basic training, we were shipped to a teachers college in Jamestown, North Dakota, to take academic training at the College Training Detachment (CTD) there. I remember the place well, especially two incidents. One morning we awoke to find our shoes missing. Two hundred pairs of shoes had been thrown helter-skelter into a barracks bag! It may have been the same jokers who later gave student officers the "brown nose" treatment by putting brown liquid shoe polish on their noses while they were sleeping. The people of Jamestown were very friendly and hospitable to us cadets; my memories of the town are fond ones.

In June 1943 our Cadet class of 44-D was ordered to Santa Ana, California, for classification and pre-flight school. I qualified as pilot or bombardier. Of course I chose to be a pilot. The day started at 5:00 a.m. and ended at 5:00 p.m.—courses in navigation, meteorology, etc. plus calisthenics, running and team sports. Joe DiMaggio was one of my instructors. After six weeks we could go off the base on leave. We would take the "red cars" into L.A. on Saturdays after 5:00 p.m., attending shows, hanging around, sleeping in movie theaters or on lawns. On Sunday mornings we marched to the parade ground, singing as we went, stopping occasionally to pound our chests and give the war cry "Hubba! Hubba! Hubba!" The frivolity gave way to discipline after we reached the parade ground where we stood at "parade rest" for stretches as long as two hours. Our squadron finished with the number one over-all rating, so we got first pick for primary flying school. We chose Cal Aero Flying Academy in Chino, close to Ontario, California. Brother John came to the same school later. He became a B-17 pilot and completed 24 missions in Europe.

After primary and basic flight training at Cal Aero, I was sent to Marfa, Texas, for Advanced. I nearly "bought the farm" on an AT-17 Cessna "bamboo bomber" one night when one engine quit at 100 feet. After I received my wings and commission I was sent to Reno for transition training in the C-47 and C-46. Those orders completely changed the course of my life, for it was in Reno that I met Neva (Billie) Gardner, the most beautiful, most unselfish, most wonderful girl in the whole world. A year and a half later, she became my wife.

On July 7, 1944, assigned copilot on a C-46, I left Miami for India. We spent five days in Khartoum waiting for a brake cylinder to be replaced. Then it was off for Karachi in western India. It was raining so hard (this was the middle of the monsoon season) we were taken from the plane by rowboat to operations and later to our sleeping quarters. The next day, luckily, the runway was not inundated so we took off for Misamari via Agra. After two days I was sent to Mohanbari. I was there until October, when I was transferred back to Misamri. From these two basses I flew 91 round-trips to bases in China over the scary Hump.

The two flights I remember most clearly are one out of Mohanbari and one out of Misamari. On my first 14 flights, I didn't get to see the Hump terrain at all. On my next flight, returning from China at night, lightening surrounded the plane. When we flew into a thunderstorm, the plane shook so violently I thought it was coming apart. Hail as big as softballs struck the fuselage. We went in at 18,000 feet and after an eternity (more like 45 seconds) were tossed out of the thunderstorm like a peanut shell at 23,000 feet.

Sometime in December, again at night, on instruments, the right engine coughed and quit. The copilot and radio operator went to the cargo door to prepare to bail out. I continued to work the mixture control and throttle. At 17,000 I was about to give the order to jump when my efforts paid off and the engine came back to life. I climbed to cruising altitude. I'm sure we had been below the tops of the Hump's high peaks, but God's hand was on our shoulder, and we survived.

Near the end of February 1945 I received orders to return stateside. We landed in Miami, took a bus in town, spotted a hamburger place and proceeded to enjoy our best meal in nearly a year—three hamburgers and two milkshakes!

I was assigned ferrying duty. Finally I was separated from the service on August 8, 1945, from the East Base at Great Falls.

For most of us, our WWII experience changed our lives forever. All four of us Watne boys survived the war. The real heroes are those who gave their lives, whether in the CBI or any other theater or place. The price of freedom is high.

Leonard Watne

▶In December 2000 Leonard wrote an account of his life from 1938 to 1947 in a spiral-back booklet he called *I'm in the Air Corps Now.* He dedicated it to his four grandsons, "who have always brought such joy to my wife and me."

Mohns Hill, PA

Dear Carl,

Do you recall when we first met as new teachers at Wilson High School? I wonder how long it was before we discovered we had both served in the CBI. While I was down below in the jungle of Burma, you flew over me nearly two hundred times on your Himalayan flights to and from China.

I spent two and a half years in a Service Squadron in that miserable land, 27 months of that time "up front," as we used to say. Our mission as quartermaster was to supply food, clothing, and gasoline. I was first assigned to run the office at Headquarters at Hellgate. Then I was sent into the field. We started there at Hellgate, then when it finally got livable, it seemed it was time to move on. That frustration was repeated many times.

Moving from one village to another was difficult for another reason. Every region had its own dialect. We had a guide who was, amazingly, a Korean. He worked for the Burmese government because even the government couldn't speak to the natives in some villages. I never found out how this Korean came to be there.

I spent most of my time at Shingbwiyang. At that base there were two engineering groups, three companies of quartermasters, and a few infantry companies. We had an emergency airstrip. Nearby Tingkwaskskan had a longer strip where C-47s, C-46s, and small bombers could land. I was also at Bhamo and Myitkyina, which were completely leveled by enemy bombing and shelling.

I didn't know why at the time, but I was selected to be the squadron guide. I was told later that I was chosen because I never got lost. I'd take a look at where the sun was and note my position. I remember on one occasion being in the jungle with a captain who had been put in charge. After a while he seemed confused. "Captain," I said, "you seem in a quandary."

"I am," he replied. "I don't know where we are."

"Give me twenty minutes," I said, "and I'll take off and find a place I can recognize." I did and we returned to our base safely.

What I remember most vividly about my jungle duty some 60 years ago was the terrible living conditions—the monsoon rains, the heat, the leeches, the mosquitoes, the slow travel in the nearly impenetrable jungle.

In all my memories, one strange incident stands out. One day while I was working toward the airstrip, I noticed a church on my right. Just as I entered, a monk in an orange-colored robe entered behind me. We knelt to pray. As we left the church, he stopped me. He raised his arms toward the sky and said, "One!" He walked a few steps and said again, "One!" Everywhere in the world, one God indeed.

Best regards,
Paul E. Strunk

Canton, OH

Dear Mr. Constein,

My husband, Ken, was a pilot stationed at Mohanbari. He is 81 and not well. Recently he has sort of given up hope. He has had cancer, a broken hip, diabetes, heart failure, and other complications.

His life was mainly flying. He taught many students how to be safe in the air.

I am enjoying your book and your journeys.

Sincerely,
Helene A. Little

▶I also received a letter from Ken Little. He referred to his wife's poetry. "She has been writing poems for about fifty years, some of them pretty darn good. Her poem about my early flying won a prize in a national contest." I consider it first-rate. Ken also told me about his 86 round-trips on the Hump, his two engine failures in the CBI, and about some soft staff missions flying to Bombay and Bangalore.

Flight, the Beginning

I was one who knifed the virgin heavens
And scattered stars.
I dreamed the dream that few men dared
And reached for Mars.
I ran familiar roughened ground,
Sat between the fragile wings;
Still earth and plane stayed welded,
For they knew not of such things.

One cloudless day I slowly lifted,
Stranger to these foreign skies;
Unshackled man, I rivaled birds;
I'd broken earthbound ties.
I topped trees and skirted clouds,
Passed the roof of heaven soon,
This journey meant to scatter stars
Had reached and touched the moon!

For I had crossed a new dimension,

Where would my journey end?
When first I'd lifted awkward wings
But to return to earth again.
Yes, I was one who dreamed the dream
That long ago began,
But as I opened skyward doors
I joined God's hand to man.

Helene Little

Germantown, OH

Hello Fellow Humpster,

Reading your memoir was like reading my own diary. I felt I was riding with you in the cockpit.

I enlisted at Patterson Field to be an Aviation Cadet. After basic training (drilling, etc.) I was sent to the Air Corp's College Training Detachment at Kutztown (PA) State Teachers College.

(▶What a coincidence! Kutztown STC is where both my wife, Amy, and I received our BS degrees, mine in 1942.)

Carl, I compliment you for being from that region. Those Pennsylvania Dutch were the greatest and nicest people I was ever around. One Sunday I was invited to the home of Paul and Ruth Luckenbill for dinner. We became good friends; Mrs. Luckenbill became my second mom. I wrote many letters to them after the war. In 1962 my wife and children and I visited her.

I got my commission and wings in the Class of 44-E at Freeman Field, Seymour, Indiana. After C-47 transition training at St. Joseph, Missouri, I was assigned brand new B-25s from the factory in Kansas City, Kansas. Then I deadheaded on a C-54 on the Crescent Run, as you did, from Miami Beach to Karachi, India. I was sent to Lal-hat to fly C-47s. After a month as 1st pilot on C-47s, I was assigned to Dergaon to haul pipe to Burma for pipeline construction. This was on C-46s. Some days I made three round-trips. My tent-mate and his crew bailed out and returned with the help of Naga natives.

My wildest ride came in a C-47 on July 17, 1945. I had been in the CBI for 10 months with about 900 hours in the theater. I had picked up a load of passengers at Chabua. Among them was a VIP—Brigadier General Lewis A. Pick, CO in charge of building the Ledo Road to join the Burma Road. First called the Stilwell Road or Pick's Pike, it was one of the greatest engineering feats of World War II.

It looked like the flight would be a gravy run down the valley to Lal-hat at 5,000 or 6,000 feet, and I was elated to have the general aboard. It turned out to be my hairiest and scariest flight ever.

We took off into the night at 2,200 hours. About 20 miles out we were unnerved to see St. Elmo's Fire on the wings and props. I slipped on the "Fasten Seat Belt" and "No Smoking" signs and took off the autopilot. The night was pitch black; all we could see was the instruments. Suddenly we hit a solid wall of water and the worst turbulence I had ever experienced. The altimeter and rate of climb went wild, and all the gauges fell below the green. I was busy calling orders to the copilot and praying at the same time. I knew the ground wasn't too far below us at times, and we were finally kicked out on top at 12,000 feet. How those trusty Pratt & Whitney engines kept going and how the wings stayed on I'll never know.

Two hours later we limped into Lal-hat practically on one engine. Some cylinder heads in the right engine had been cracked, probably due to the sudden cold-water bath.

Totally I flew 387 trips to 24 fields or strips all over India and Burma. Whenever we got to Chabua, where you were based, we always remarked that it was probably the worst base and had the toughest flight schedule in the CBI. So glad you made it, Carl. I thank the Lord each night before retiring that he saw fit to let me make it from that "Russian Roulette."

As you did, I left for home aboard ship from Karachi in November 1945. I came home to farm with my father and to marry Janet, the girl I left behind. We will celebrate our fifty-sixth wedding anniversary on May 4, 2002. I have retired from farming because of arthritis, and I no longer am able to attend reunions of the Hump Pilots Association.

Your Fellow Hump Pilot,
Billy D. Rogers

Weatogue, CT

Dear Carl,

I enjoyed your book. And talk about coincidences! From the same Miami hotel, the Floridian, I flew the identical route you did to India, even to a stopover in Bermuda because of engine trouble. If it had been September (1944) instead of October, I would have guessed we were on the same plane.

I was a member of the first direction-finding teams of the CBI. After obtaining radio fixes on a "lost" plane over the Hump, we would plot a bearing on a large map and tell the pilots their position. Often during the monsoons there were several planes lost at the same time. We would stay with them until they found their way.

I was at all the places you mentioned—the Azores, Casablanca, Tripoli, Cairo, Abadan, Karachi, Agra, Chabua, Calcutta, Kunming—during my duty in the CBI. I worked the longest at Kurmitola/Tezgaon. I remember your base, Chabua, well—it rained all the time.

I flew the Hump once as a radio operator. In my rush to get aboard, I forgot to take a parachute. Fortunately, I didn't realize my mistake until late in the trip.

After the war I entered Harvard and earned a degree in economics. Then I joined a company few people recognized then—IBM. I had a lifetime career there, retiring in 1982.

Many thanks,
Irv Knight

►Of course our crews were never lost—we were just "uncertain of our position." More than once the triangulation fellows got me back safely.

Plymouth, WI

►The most beautiful letter I received—literally beautiful—came from Harvey Borkenhagen.

Carl

Thought I should send these pages to you.
I have attached a set like these to the
inside of your book. My kids are overjoyed.

What a pleasant surprise reading Constein's book, "The Hump". In June of 2000 I received a postcard from him telling me about this book. I'm sure he got my address from the roster of the Hump Pilots Association. I knew his book would be describing his experiences in flying the Hump but what I didn't know was that our careers in the Air Corps were very similar. He received his pilot's wings on Aug 4, 1944 at Blackland Field, Waco, Texas the same day and same place I received mine!! We were in the same class! Did I know him then? I don't remember.

He describes his days as a cadet before he became pilot. What a similarity. He went to College training Detachment as did I. He to University of Toledo and I to Xavier University in Cincinnati. He says his CTD was a soft touch for six weeks. Not mine. I spent 5 months of intensified subjects like Math, Meterology, physics, etc. In addition, the physical training was as vigorous as could be, featuring one hour of muscle wrenching calisthenics every day to a 6mile run three days a week, in formation, and singing those robust songs like "Its a Grand Old Flag, Alouetta" etc through the streets and neighborhoods of Norwalk, Ohio. After CTD he was sent to San Antonio Separation Center. I was there too! — and at the same time. After that we both went to pilot training in the PT-19, then the BT-13, then the AT-17 to graduation day. His PT training was in Uvalde, Tx, mine in Ft. Worth. His BT-13 training was in Waco, mine in Brady. (where Doris and I were married) But at Advance, in the AT-17, we were in the same field, Waco, Texas. What a coincidence. He eventually went to C-46 traing and I to C-47 training. Like him I, too, was a victim of screwed up orders. After graduation I was sent to Reno for C-46 training but soon learned it was a mistake and subsequently was sent to B-24 school in Ft. Worth. This, too, was a mistake. The minimum weight for a B-24 was 160 — I think I weighed 155 or so. Then onto St. Joseph, MO for C-47 training - then to Nashville, the port of Embarkation. He was there too! Then to Miami, Belem, Natal and then the tiny island of Ascension, to the Gold Coast of Africa, all the way thru Africa, Egypt, the Aden Sea, Karachi, Agra and finally to China. This was the Southern route. Constein went the Northern route thru the Azores Islands.

Flying the Himalyas (the Hump) was as dangerous as he says. The perils being bad weather, high winds, poor radio reception and for us C-47 jockeys, the lack of a safe altitude. Because the C-47 was smaller and less powered than the C-46 we always fought for altitude. He cruised a good 6000 feet higher than we could and boy, at our altitude those mountains were big, and high, because of down drafts. He described that terrible night of Jan 6. The night when many planes went down because of extreme weather, thunderstorms and ice. I also flew that night. We left our home base of Chanyi and landed at Kunming (about 80 miles) for a load to fly to Burma. Arriving at Operations there the talk was about the severe weather over the Hump as many who just made the trip were milling around swapping stories; like how lucky they were to have survived it. Finally the word came out the Hump was closed and everybody shouted for joy.

My duties were much like his, to fly personnel, supplies, and gasoline (on most trips) from Burma and India to points all thru China. One time we flew 48 hours straight evacuating Gen. Stillwell's army from the Ledo Road in Burma to the front in China. Can you imagine the smell in the airplane loaded with garlic eating Chinese? Our most disliked cargo was horses. While flying at altitude all was well but coming in to land, on the approach, if one horse would lean to the side we had to immediately get the wing up on that side to regain stability – no fun!

Out of my outfit only two of us reached the required amount of flying hours and was sent back to the US in plush C-54s. All the other guys remained at base, loading equipment, supplies etc into trucks and them driving them to Kunming over very poor roads. Hey! these were pilots, driving trucks! Then they were sent back to the states, by boat!

My trip back home took me thru Baghdad, Cairo, Tripoli, Casablanca, the Azores and then NY City. I was assigned to the Ferry Command but instead of flying all different kinds of aircraft I was stuck with the NAVY PBY, which was named the OA-10, the army version. Stationed at Long Beach I rode Military Air Transport to Spokane – picked up the OA-10s (I made three trips) and delivered them to Kelly Field in San Antonio where other ferry pilots delivered them to So. America their ultimate destination.

After a few months at Long Beach it became time to decrease the number of pilots in the service. We were given three options: one to walk across the field and take jobs as airline pilots for Slick Airlines, two to sign up for an additional four years of duty, or three, to get out. I elected to get out because I wanted to go to Veterinary school. Therefore, on Sept 9, 1946 I received my discharge at Beale Air Force Base, California.

I thank Constein for his book describing the life I lived so many years ago. It brought back many memories long forgotten.

Wilmington, NC

Dr. Constein,

I was in the first group of twenty-six C-46 pilots to be assigned to the Assam, India, base at Sookerating. We replaced the original Hump pilots who did their best to fly cargo to China in the smaller C-47, flying only during daylight hours in fairly good weather. With our "Ole Dumbos" we flew around the clock in all kinds of weather at altitudes high enough to clear Himalayan peaks as high as 16,000 feet. On one flight I lost the right engine and returned from Kunming on one engine at 12,000 feet.

After I had made 75 round-trip Hump flights to China, I flew with the C-47 Troop Carrier Group based at Sookerating in transporting Chinese troops from Ledo to Myitkyina (MISH-in-awe) in order to relieve Merrill's Marauders, who had just captured the northern end of the airfield there. I recall my first flight on this assignment.

The crew chief of the C-47 Gooney Bird of our assigned plane asked to go with us. I asked the other pilot to take the first takeoff and landing since I hadn't flown the 47 for a year. He replied, "That's more than I can say for myself. I have never flown the 47 at all!" I understood why the crew chief backed out, mumbling something about taking care of a problem in the hanger.

Fifty years later I learned that a high school classmate, Richard Dixon, who was billeted only one block from me in Burma in the area known as Drypond, was killed that same day by a Japanese sniper as Dixon worked on a tractor grading the runway.

It's a small, small world.

John William "Jack" Loughlin
Lt. Col. USAF Retired

▶Unlike most veterans who decry their loss of memory, Lt. Col. Loughlin claims his is good. He has copies of all his military orders and his complete Form 5 flight records. He hopes to write about his experiences on the Hump, even if it never gets published. I encourage him and all veterans to get it down on paper. As for publishing—it's easier than it once was.

Bern Township, PA

Dear Carl,

I enlisted in the Army Air Corps in February 1941. After doing assignments in ground transportation with the 89th Material Squadron at Maxwell Field, AL, Moultrie, GA, and Waterboro, SC, I became Assistant Truckmaster. We were part of the 305th Service Group and set sail on October 7, 1942, for parts unknown aboard the RMS Mauretania. *At Port Said 5,000 GIs disembarked—but not us. Five hundred German prisoners came aboard and the ship sailed back down the Red Sea and across the Indian Ocean to Columbo, Ceylon. We were then transshipped to Bombay. That was in early December. After two days of sightseeing, we boarded a troop train for a month in Agra. I enjoyed visiting the Taj Mahal and the Red Fort.*

In January 1943 the 305th left Agra for the town of Ondal, India, where we opened a new base for 3rd Echelon repair work. I was promoted to tech sergeant and put in charge of the heavy equipment Motor Pool. We had 2 and ½-ton autocar tractors and 7 and ½-ton C2 wreckers used to haul back wrecked planes. We were very busy. In June I caught a break from the extreme heat of Ondal when I got two weeks' R&R in Ranikhet, high in the Himalayas. Later a group of us was sent to Dum Dum Airport in Calcutta to uncrate P- 43s and remove the instruments. What remained of the planes was junked. I have no idea why. What I recall most about that trip was going to the Winter Garden after dinner to dance. The popular song White Christmas *was played over and over again.*

In January 1944 the 89th was separated from the 305th and sent to Tezgaon to open a new base. We became part of the newly arrived 54th Service Group. It was here that we assembled L-5s and gliders for Col. Cochran's push into Burma. I recall one crew chief saying, "If I am going to put this thing together, I'm going to fly it." Which he did one Sunday afternoon. He was busted to private and restricted to base for three months. Another sergeant got the same punishment when he was ordered to test a box of flare guns. He stepped out the front door and shot up a flare, which landed on the thatched roof of the supply room. It created one big, beautiful fire, consuming the building and its contents.

What I remember best about Tezgaon was the crash of a P-38 one Sunday afternoon. A group of us NCOs quartered in the "City Hall Basha" were about to go to the mess hall. Suddenly we heard the unmistakable roar of a P-38 in a power dive. In a little while we heard the roar again and waited for the pilot to pull up again. We stopped talking and waited breathlessly. Sgt. Evenski cried out, "My God, he's going to hit, he's going to hit!" The pilot had come in too low on his second dive, clipped a tree, hit the ground between the dayroom and the dispensary, killing a GI, then plowing through the mess hall and exiting through the outer wall. A number of others were saved only because they were seated along the inner wall. But some of them were badly burned. Had this happened 45 minutes later, it would have caught the 89th lined up for chow and wiped out most of the squadron.

Toward the end of 1944, after Germany had been defeated, we learned that we would be sent back to the States on points. The EM Club decided to use up its substantial treasury by sponsoring a free dinner and inviting the officers. After the dinner we all proceeded to the Club, where two wash tubs had been filled with the gin that remained, lime, and soda. "Help yourselves, men. Use your mess cup." The last thing I remember of that night was talking with my CO, Major Ramsey, about my post-war plans.

In January my 1st sergeant informed me I was going home. In a way, it was a sad occasion because I was leaving a group of men I'd been with for almost four years. They were like brothers to me. I left Bombay aboard the US General Randall *and sailed across the Pacific to San Pedro, California. One memory from that voyage that has stayed with me to this day was the song "Lili Marlene" sung every single day and night for 30 days. If I ever have a daughter, I said to myself, I'll name her Marlene.*

After docking in San Pedro, I was sent by troop train to Ft. Dix, N.J. After a furlough, I was ordered to Greenville, SC, Air Base. There I met the girl who was to become my wife. We were married in September.

In October I was discharged from the service at Mitchel Field, Long Island. I had spent four years, eight months, and seven days in the Air Corps/Air Force—and I never regretted a day of it. In my overseas travel I circumnavigated the globe and crossed the Equator four times.

We stayed in Greenville. I went to work in a cotton mill as an electrician. Our first daughter was born in September 1947. We named her Sheilagh Marlene. (Sheilagh was the name of a girl whose mother worked in the US Consul's office in Calcutta. I had promised myself to use that name as well for a daughter.) We moved to Queens, Long Island, where I worked for the Bulova Watch Company.

In 1946 I achieved a life-long dream of owning a farm. I sold the Pennsylvania gem in 1970 but kept two acres on which to build a home. After working for 15 years at nearby Hofmann Industries, and after that in a small shop close to home, I retired completely in 1999 at the age of 83.

In 1972 I became active in the China-Burma-India Veterans Association. In 1981 I organized the Great Valley Basha and continue to serve as editor-publisher the Basha newsletter. On the national level I served in various capacities, including national commander in 1993.

At 85, I consider that I have had a good life—a loving wife, three children, eight grandchildren, four great grandchildren. When anyone asks me how I feel, my response is, "There is nothing wrong with me that hitting the lottery won't cure."

Good luck,
Louis R. Porto

Ashland, OR

Dr. Constein,

I spent a little time in C-46s—in the cargo compartment where EMs belong. I was not a crew member but occasionally went on 4th Combat Cargo Group flights to deliver cargo to strips in Burma during the Central Burma Campaign. The Meiktila trip was a bit hairy because fighting was still going on there.

I was assigned to the 382nd Air Service Group in Chittagong where the 4th C C G operated. Later I took the "low route" over the Hump, driving a weapons carrier across the Burma Road. Our group had been reassigned to Liuchow, China. After the war ended, we were moved to Shanghai for a couple months, then home.

Thanks for sending your memoir.

Charlie Booth

Edgewood, KY

Dear Dr. Constein,

I was one of 29 S/Sgt pilots who arrived in India on December 5, 1942, to fly the Hump. I was stationed at Chabua, then Mohanbari, later Tezpur, and finally Misamari. I had the distinction of being the first S/Sgt pilot to check out in the C-46 and only one of two to ever fly the aircraft over the Hump as an enlisted man.

I'm looking forward to reading your book.

Sincerely,
Charlie Plummer

Endicott, NY

Dear Dr. Constein:

I received your book, gift of my good friend Irv Knight. Irv and I were part of a group of young men at Hamilton College in Clinton, New York, studying to become weather officers. The program folded and we were thrown into the US Army Air Corps. We went through a three-month course in direction finding then prepared to go overseas.

In September 1944 I left Miami on a C-46 bound for Natal, Brazil. I spent three weeks there, and then flew in a C-107 to Ascension Island, then Accra on the Gold Coast of Africa. We hop-scotched across Africa in a C-47. When we got to Aden, I was so air sick I was taken off the shipment and spent six days in a hospital. I later caught up with my group in Karachi. Again, a problem. I spent three weeks in Chabua in the hospital recovering from maleria. The group headed for Kweilin, China, but the base had been evacuated and the landing strip blown up in anticipation of a take-over by the Japanese. We ended up in Kurmitola.

Our job in India was to locate lost aircraft by means of triangulation. So far as I know, our team never lost a plane.

Before the war I spent a weekend in your home town in the fall of 1942. I was a freshman at Franklin and Marshall College in Lancaster. One of my closest friends there was Dick Kleppinger of Fleetwood. I'm sure you remember him and his father's grocery and hardware store. Dick was an outstanding basketball player and all-round athlete. In your book you referred to a Gus Riemondi. I met his sister when I visited your town. Two of my other friends were Don Huyett and Bob Lacey. I believe Bob was from nearby Birdsboro. Small world.

Very truly yours,
Anthony "Ted" Clemente

▶Of course I remember the Kleppingers, the Riemondis, the Huyetts, and Bob Lacey. I remember most families in our little town.

Concord, CA

Dear Compatriot,

I flew 60 trips over the Hump from Sookerating but got credit for only 59 because the report of my last trip, together with my application to stay in the army, got lost.

I was an instructor at Cal Aero in Ontario, California, before signing up for ATC in Long Beach. When I arrived at Sook, I was assigned to the 3rd Air Transport Squadron as F/O attached to the 20th Air Force. I flew the last plane out of Sookerating when the base closed.

On a cargo flight to China one night I was flying copilot for Zac. When the field at our destination closed because of an accident, Zac lost his bearings and got us lost. He took the radio operator's seat and began calling for help. Our fuel was getting low, and I decided to jump out at the next time I saw light on the ground. Just then a radio operator at a fighter base heard Zac's call and answered. They sent up flares. Zac returned to the pilot's seat and prepared to land at the fighter base. He failed three times to make a landing approach. I took over, got him lined up and let him land. When we finally cut the engines, he got out of the plane, got down on his hands and knees and kissed the ground.

On another occasion, in a bar in Indianapolis one night I overheard a Chicken Colonel say to his buddy, "Boy, he must have screwed up, a flight officer in the 20th?" I know you understand, but many people do not—a Flight Officer was equal in rank to a Second Lieutenant.

Excuse the poor handwriting. I had a stroke in '87, heart surgery in '89, left knee replaced in '91. I'll be 87 in October.

Orlo R. Watson

Aurora, OH

Dear Dr. Constein:

Your military career, also starting in the Army, was pretty much conventional and successful. Mine began quite differently. I received my initial flight training in a J-3 Cub, qualifying for the Civilian Pilot Training Program. I received a private pilot license and went into the Air Force Reserve. Next came Secondary Training in a Meyers OTW biplane roughly similar to a Stearman. I loved the aerobatics. This was followed by cross country navigation training at the Akron Airport, and then intensive Commercial Flight Instructor Training, mostly in a Waco UPF-7. I had a superb instructor who whipped me into shape.

Then came an order to report to Montgomery, Alabama, at my own expense. Several hundred of us were permitted to select a contract flying school of the Southeast Training Command where we would train aviation cadets to fly, from scratch. I didn't like the job, although I loved flying a Stearman, in spite of its tendency to ground loop. (I did this with my very first student.) After a year I had a belly full and hoped to become a civilian basic instructor in California. When I got there, the offering had closed down.

At the same time the Ferry Command accepted a number of us surplus primary instructors for Basic Training at Deming, NM, and for Officer Candidate School Training at Nashville as civilians! We ignored and laughed at orders like "fall out for PT." Hardly qualified for the military, we made it through in about thirty days. Low and behold, the whole group graduated and became Service Pilot Flight Officers. WOW! My best buddy and I selected single engine fighter ferrying training at Brownsville, Texas. After soloing from the rear seat of an AT-6, it was great fun. I got to fly them all, but no funny stuff like aerobatics. A few nuts killed themselves trying to fly under bridges or shooting the cannon in a P-63, a large version of a P-39 with the Russian Red Star insignia.

To my amazement, the Ferry Command allowed each of us to choose a home base. My Chicago friend Tony and I selected Romulus, Michigan, the closest base to our homes. We often made unauthorized stops at our hometowns. The dream job, unfortunately, lasted only three months. We were abruptly ordered to Homestead, Florida, to train as B-24 copilots. Without knowing it, we were destined for the "Hump."

I must back up here. As flight instructors at Lakeland, Florida, we had to fight off the girls, a new experience for this naïve guy. Tony, whom I still see after fifty-five years, is still married to Margaret. I struck out and could take only seven years of the unfaithful bitch before kicking her out. I must say I envy the mutual love and compassion you and your wife shared. I kicked around for ten years, happily single, until I met my present wife, an old-fashioned girl and a member of a group of single people where I wound up as president. We have the same fine values although we come from opposite ends of the religious rainbow—still getting along well after thirty-eight years with a daughter (Stanford Masters Mechanical Engineer with a great husband and three kids) and my son, now my boss, with a daughter and a son. And five wonderful grandchildren. WOW! What great luck!

So you and I wound up with similar flying careers flying the Hump. A bit of a rebel, I was threatened with a court martial three times for "smart aleck conduct" or resisting orders which made no sense. At 81 I'm still working full time manufacturing industrial brushes, still doing aerobatics. Your book triggered a lifetime of wonderful memories.

Sincerely,
Lloyd P. Benjamin

Lloyd Benjamin (third from right) with his Primary Flight students in the class of 43-G, Lakeland, Florida. The plane is a Stearman.

Grove City, OH

Dear Dr. Constein:

I was a pilot stationed at Mohanbari from January 1945 to December 1945. I made 101 round-trip Hump flights in C-46s, plus 40- some hours in the valley. In the last three months of my stay at Mohanbari I was Chief Pilot, which I considered quite an honor.

Upon my return to the states, I was stationed at Westover Field in Chicopee Falls, Massachusetts. Until my discharge in June 1948 I flew C-54s to Paris, Frankfort, and Rome.

I graduated from Cadet school in Valdosta, Georgia, with the class of 42-I.

The best of luck with your book. I think every Hump pilot should read it, especially those pilots like you and me who were stationed in the Upper Assam Valley.

Sincerely,
Coleman Cook

Bartlesville, OK

Dr. Carl Frey Constein

I'm Chilton Gates and I arrived at Chabua New Year's Eve 1945, just before the January 6-7 big loss of planes and crew. I made one trip before that and luckily was on the ground that night. What have I got myself in for? I thought.

When I got there we could fly 500 hours then go home. Then it went to 650, then 750 and stay one year. If you had 500 hours when they changed it to 750, you flew your 650 then went home. I was short 50 hours so I had to stay a year and fly 750. I didn't get it—some went by hours, some by trips.

Here in Bartlesville we have about twenty Hump/CBI guys who meet once a week to shoot the breeze and once a month for a meal with a speaker of some kind. They thought it would be nice if you could make it to one of our meetings or picnics some time. Our next picnic is on Friday, October 13. You can see we are not superstitious. Hope the WX cools down by then.

Thanks a lot,
Chilton Gates

South Weymouth, MA

Dear Dr. Constein,

Your book tickled my memory and brought back many experiences. Each time I subsequently picked it up I recalled something else. For example, when you wrote of the one takeoff-one landing check ride we got in the C-46, I recall saying to myself, "That is not enough experience in an unfamiliar aircraft for a Hump trip the next day." So I called the tower and got an ok for a training flight (out of Dinjan). Then I got into that big bird all alone and proceeded to shoot some landings. The next day I felt a bit more comfortable about having a crew on board.

I graduated from cadets (44-F) about the same time you did, but my experience was quite different. From advanced flight school, we were sent to transition school for C-47s and gliders. This took about four months. Then we were each "issued" a brand-new C-47, for which we had to pay $1.00! Orders were cut for me to fly the 47 from Ft. Wayne, Indiana, to Shingbwiang, where I joined the 2nd Troop Carrier Squadron and proceeded to fly drop missions into southern Burma. In June of '45 we were sent to Dinjan where we proceeded to fly the Hump until about September. When the war ended we got involved in China's civil war, flying missions against Mao and his Communists until December, when we came home from Shanghai to LA aboard an aircraft carrier.

Back home in the states, I spent a year flying A-26s, doing air shows around the country. After that it was back to college (Brown University) on the GI Bill.

Your book is valuable to me because, unlike you, I did not document my experiences. I tried to get my Form 5 flight records but was told all such records were lost in a fire in a St. Louis warehouse. Do you suppose some other agency microfilmed the records prior to the fire?

I hope to meet you at the Hump Pilots Association convention in DC in August.

Sincerely,
Lewis R. Sheldon Jr.

P. S. Excuse my typos. I don't yet know how to go back and make corrections in the middle of a page.

Schofield, WI

Dear Dr. Constein,

My father, who passed away last year, also flew the Hump. He used to tell us stories and show us pictures he took in India and China. I'm hoping your book will give us a better insight into what you all had to go through. Not enough is ever said about the forgotten heroes who risked their lives every day flying the Hump. I even have friends who never even heard about it. My father said more planes were lost on the Hump than in the 8th Air Force

Good health to you.

Sincerely,
Tom Bartelme

Wyomissing, PA

Dear Carl,

Here's a tale of coincidence for you. Of course you know Wendall Phillips, national chaplain and past national commander of the CBI Veterans Association. Well, Wendall stopped in recently to buy a new car.

He urged me to attend the dinner-meeting of the local Great Valley Basha to be held at a restaurant just down the street from my dealership. During our conversation, I told Wendall I had been an ATC C-46 pilot stationed in Chengkung.

"I was stationed there too," Wendall said. "I was a radio operator."

"Really?" I said. "Well, I owe my life to one radio operator who got me home when I was lost on a tough flight."

"It's possible I was that guy," Wendall said, and left in his new car.

At the CBI dinner the following Sunday, Wendall approached me and said, "Yep, I was your radio man. All I did was get a radio fix from three stations and give you the heading home to Chengkung. Here's a copy of my log." His flight record showed: "August 2, 1945—C-46A #216; DB-IM-DB—5 hours, 10 minutes."

"I'll be damn," I recall saying. "I'm going to check for my log at home. I'm not sure I have it."

Sure enough, there it was, stuffed in my old WWII briefcase on the attic. The August 2 entry was exactly as Wendall had reported it. After that scary flight I was just 77 hours short of every Hump pilot's goal of 750 hours and home!

That August 2 flight was scary—but perhaps not as scary as a close call on the ground at Kunming, China. We had come in from Kurmitola and were instructed where to park our C-109. As we were taxiing we heard a tremendous roar. We thought a plane had landed on a taxi-strip. It would not have been the first time that happened. But not this time. What really happened was that a C-46 lost its brakes, and the pilot tried to maneuver by accelerating one engine. He rammed into the tail section of our Flying Gas Tank and removed 20 feet of the plane!

As you know, Carl, the C-109 tanker was a converted B-24 bomber, with four 600-gallon tanks installed in the bombardier compartment, a 300-gallon tank behind the bomb bay, and another 300-gallon tank elsewhere—this in addition to 2,000 gallons of gasoline in the wing tanks. Crews were not allowed to smoke or use the heaters. To vent fumes, the bomb bay doors were kept partially open. All this weighed heavily on our minds as we saw oil splattering in all directions and heard a scary hissing sound coming from our oxygen tanks. We shut down the engines immediately, threw open the hatch, and scrambled into the revetment, all the time waiting for an explosion. It never came! The gasoline had been delivered to China as planned.

The demand for gasoline by our forces in China was great. One problem the ATC faced was a long turn-around time for unloading cargo, feeding the crew, and getting flight clearance for the return to India. While I was operations officer at Chengkung, I talked to some on the incoming pilots about reducing the turn-around time. (Two pilot-friends from home who flew into the base while I was there were John Schach and Ed Angstadt, the latter deceased.) On a chalkboard I wrote the name of the pilot, his home base, and his turn-around time. We started with 45 minutes. Each crew that flew in determined to beat that time, and every day the time dropped.

Finally on an August 1945 day when there was NO WIND, in a coordinated effort with the Chengkung base, an approaching crew radioed in that they were going for a record. As they landed and rolled down the runway, the engineer unlocked the twenty-six 55-gallon drums of gasoline, the plane came to a stop and the engineer quickly threw open the cargo door, and the rest of the crew rolled the barrels unto a waiting truck. Our field personnel came on board and handed a clearance for the pilot, copilot, and engineer. The left engine had not been shut down. When all was clear, the tower gave its clearance, the pilot started the right engine, turned the plane around and took off in the opposite direction. There was NO WIND. Turn-around time? Eight minutes! Major Rittenberry, our CO, was proud but cautioned us concerning safety. In his book, the Hump CO, General Tunner, stated that the record was 13 minutes. We believe ours was the world record.

If anyone who reads this book was a crew member on that turn-around or was trying for a record in 1945 in Chengkung, China, I hope he will write and tell you so you can pass his name on to me.

Let's get together soon.
Tom Masano

Ft. Worth, TX

Dear Carl,

I too was flying the Hump for over two years between December '43 and October '45. I was not a pilot but a flight engineer/crew chief on a B-24 we named "Noisy Rosie." But I also flew as flight mechanic on C-46s and C-109s. I had some good flights, some scary flights, and, if the weather was clear (not often), some flights with beautiful scenery—and closer to God!

Please send me a copy of your book ASAP. I am retired now and have time to read and loaf and take orders from my wife.

God Bless,
Hector Beltram

▶ I had crew chiefs on board more frequently on my earlier flights. I never understood—and of course no one explained—how it was determined that they were assigned to some flights but not others.

West Hartford, CT

Dear Dr. Constein,

I was in the ATC stationed at Misamari in Assam Province from October 6, 1943, to December 1, 1945, as an enlisted man. I worked in headquarters, making all kinds of reports to Calcutta. I want to comment on your book.

p. 12 Who could have believed that years later our Commander-in-Chief would be charged with lying under oath and obstructing justice, would be impeached, and would say that impeachment wasn't so bad. As a veteran, as an American, I am deeply offended and saddened by the President's conduct and low moral standards. I agree a thousand percent. My wife and I are from Arkansas. We think the man is awful and void of character. When we meet new people now and they ask where we are from, I get a kick out of my wife's reply—Texas! In my view, Clinton is the worst President this country has ever had. How can our children look up to and honor this man?

p. 31 Captain Slattery was a prototype chickenshit. One night I was standing in the road in a huge rainstorm, trying to hitch a ride back to my basha. A jeep stopped and I got in. The captain said, "Don't you salute officers? Get out and salute me and I'll tell you when to get back in." I do not believe the captain was a pilot.

p. 37 It's a Long, Long Way We flew across the desert to Cairo and then to Abadan. I agree Abadan (Iran) is the hottest place I'd ever visited.

It was a lend-lease base: the Russians came there to pick up the equipment and take it back to Russia.

p. 62 The moment of takeoff, not landing, was the moment I feared, the crucial moment of every flight in a C-46, so prone to engine failure. When I first got to Misamari, before my job assignment I was on guard duty on the runway. One night here comes a C-46 down the strip on takeoff. It was barely off the ground when it went down in a fiery explosion. They did not get another flight off until the next morning. I thought they made the right decision not to allow planes to take off over that fire.

p. 99 I don't recall a USO troupe or entertainment of any kind at Chabua. At Misamari we were lucky to have had at least one USO show—Jinx Falkenberg—she was very pretty—Melvyn Douglas and musicians.

p. 127 Going Home! We also went home by ship from Karachi via the Suez Canal and the Mediterranean. At home we had tasty food for the first time in years. Incidentally, you never mentioned eating Spam. It seems we had it every single day!

I thank you for writing an excellent book.

Have a Merry Christmas,
Gilbert M. Eddins

Brooklyn, NY

Dear Dr. Constein:

I am purchasing your book in memory of my father, Richard E. "Dick" Bran. He was an ATC pilot with the 1139th & 1140th AAFBU, stationed out of Chengkung, Luliang, and Kunming. He flew a C-47 over China/Burma/India in 1944. He passed away on June 11, 2001, but I know he would have sent for your book if he were still with us. It seems so ironic that your postcard announcing the book arrived a few days after his death.

My father did his training in Arkansas. He was such an excellent pilot that they kept him in Arkansas as an instructor. He told me he actually got down on his knees in front of the commander and begged to be sent overseas. However, he did not get his wish until 1944 when he finally got his orders and was sent to China. (Of course, this did not go over very well with my mother, as they were newlyweds.)

I will never forget the many harrowing experiences he described to me flying over those treacherous mountains. One in particular is when he was coming back from a mission and he was flying copilot. They flew into a horrendous storm over the mountains (which he said happened frequently). My father took over at the last minute and was able to bring the plane safely to base.

Another story my father told me happens to be very funny. It was late at night and he could not sleep. My father was keeping an eye on a rat that kept creeping out of a hole in the wall. Finally, my father took out his gun, aimed, and fired! There was a soldier sleeping in the next bunk. You can imagine his reaction! He jumped out of bed expecting the enemy to be at the door. My father was hysterical laughing, but he said the soldier was not too happy. I wonder why? And after all that, he missed the rat!

I intend to keep his memories alive through his stories and now your book. My sister and I miss him terribly, but my consolation is that he is now with my mother and older sister, who passed away in 1994 and 1996, respectively.

It is unfortunate that today's generation has no idea the sacrifices your generation made for this country.

Sincerely,
Barbara Parisi
Proud daughter of
Richard E. Bran, Member
Hump Pilots Association

Frederick, MD

Dear Carl,

You and I had some similarities in our WWII experiences, starting with our first assignments as MPs. Mine came about in this way.

Rolled up in my diploma from the University of Maryland in 1936 was a 2nd Lieutenant's commission in the US Army Reserves, the happy result of my enrollment in ROTC. I was called to active duty as a 1st Lieutenant in May of 1941 at Camp Lee, Virginia. Because I was the tallest of the seven who showed up at the same time, I was made an MP. I didn't like the assignment, but it was certainly better than your deal—guarding coal piles at the electric company in Philadelphia.

After a year I was able to transfer to the War Department in the Pentagon while it was under construction. I recall hand-delivering a message to a young Brigadier General by the name of Eisenhower. From there I transferred to the Army Air Corps, choosing an assignment in Physical Training, for which I was trained. I was sent to the 1st Air Force at Mitchel Field, Long Island. Then came my time to go overseas.

Together with 6,000 other troops, I boarded the brand-new troop ship the Admiral Benson for a thirty day "cruise" to India. The most memorable event was a three-day monster storm south of Australia. We arrived in Bombay and boarded a train for a four-day ride across India to Calcutta. To go with our C and K rations we got hot water from the steam locomotives for instant coffee, soup, and tea. We got off the train at a tent camp called Kanchapara outside Calcutta. I had a lot of free time to visit Calcutta, where we could stay at the Great Eastern Hotel, visit the Officers Club, attend cricket matches, and visit the Red Cross Club. I took a Red Cross tour, which included the burning gats where Hindus cremated the dead, and the Black Hole of Calcutta. Clear in my memory are the filth, poverty, and overpopulation.

My next trip was a three-day train ride through Bengal to Chabua, Assam. We changed trains and rail gauges three times and had a ferry ride across the broad Bramaputra River. After three days in Chabua, I was put aboard a C-46 for the last leg of my journey. In the middle of the night, oxygen masks on our faces, my buddies and I sat in bucket seats and, with no heat in the cabin, nearly froze to death. The ceiling of the C-46 was not as high as some of those snow-capped Himalayan peaks. All we could do was pray that the kids flying the plane knew how to fly around and over the mountains on their route. (Later I had a second flight over the Hump—from China to Calcutta and back in the nose of a B-25. Of all my memories of World War Two, the east to west flight stands out. It was a clear, beautiful day and from the best seat in the plane I got a marvelous view of the Burma jungle and the highest, most awesome mountains in the world.)

Finally I was settled in my permanent base, 14th Air Force Headquarters in Kunming, Yunnan Province, China. I was there all the time that you were flying your 96 round-trips. We were astounded that you men were flying in such lousy weather. We used to say you guys were flying when the gulls on the lake were grounded. Our pilots also flew in some bad weather, but their big hazard was Japanese planes and also anti-aircraft fire. Some of the B-24 missions took as much as twelve hours.

As Special Services Officer, I was in charge of PT. The first baseman on our softball team bailed out on one B-24 mission didn't return for two months.

The 14th Air Force was an efficient combat unit and gave the Japanese plenty of trouble. The CO, General Claire Chennault, had gone to China in 1937 to advise the Chinese Air Force. He recruited Army and Navy pilots trained at places like Pensacola, Florida, and AF bases in Texas for the American Volunteer Group, the Flying Tigers, to protect the Burma Road and defend China. Under Chennault they were an effective unit, shooting down 12 Japanese planes for each plane they lost. After Pearl Harbor, the AVG eventually became the 14th Air Force, headquartered in Kunming.

The time I spent in Kunming was a very positive experience—good weather, an interesting job, great people to work with, and a wonderful girl friend. I was lucky; several close friends of mine never made it back home.

As the war neared its end, I took over as SSO of the 14th and later moved to Chungking to become SSO of the AFCT (Air Forces in the China Theatre) as the 10th Air Force moved to China from India. On one memorable day the officers of the Headquarters were invited to a pleasant afternoon with Generalissimo and Madam Chiang Kai-Shek at their place in the country. He spoke no English but of course the Madam did, having been educated in the United States. She was a lovely, gracious lady.

Japan surrendered and our headquarters moved to Shanghai. While I was there we took over a racetrack as a recreation center and the dog track as stadium and ran a softball tournament and an Army-Navy football game.

As you did, I was sent home by troop ship. Mine, the General Scott, docked in Seattle around Christmas time. I arrived in Ft. Meade in January 1946.

I hope you were interested in my WWII experiences.

Best regards,
Warren R. Evans

▶Sounds like a different war to me! I envy Warren one thing—the freedom to visit so many interesting venues and cities in China. I flew into China 96 times, but I was never once allowed to visit a Chinese city.

Bethlehem, PA

Dear Carl,

In May of 1944 I left Norfolk, Virginia, aboard the troop ship Gen. Buckner for parts unknown. All I knew for certain was that we would be replacing infantry troops somewhere in the world. It turned out that our destination was Ramgarh, India. There we were told we had just "volunteered" to replace men from Merrill's Marauders who were being rotated home. Our group, the New Galahad, was to replace some of the original Galahad contingent of 3,000 infantrymen who arrived in India in early November 1943.

Let me go back to the origin of General Frank Merrill's Marauders. At the Quebec Conference, Prime Minister Churchill had asked President Roosevelt to get him a force of volunteers for guerrilla fighting in Burma behind Japanese lines. The Allies had been chased out of Burma by the Japanese and vowed to return. Keep in mind that the Japanese were a strong, experienced force, having invaded Manchuria a decade earlier. But the Marauders, together with British Chindits, led by General Orde Wingate, and Chinese troops trained by General Vinegar Joe Stilwell's American staff fought back, advancing from Ramgarh to northern Burma.

Fighting in the dense jungle of Burma was extremely treacherous. Fortunately, natives from the Kachin and Naga tribes aided us as guides. There were tough skirmishes all along the jungle in villages like Ledo, Walawbu, Inkangawtaung, Nhpunga, Shadazup. Many men were killed by bansi attacks and by snipers. The worst fear was not the enemy himself but the suspense of not knowing from one moment to the next when you'd run into him.

General Stilwell was determined to capture the important north Burma city of Myitkyina and build an airbase there for bombing Japan. The monsoon rains came. The Japanese built fortified foxholes; it took three months of brutal fighting to finally capture the city. The battle had taken its toll on Galahad. In addition, there were dysentery and other diseases and mental exhaustion. There was a severe breakdown of morale, almost a disintegration.

After the battle we set up a tent camp 15 miles from Myitkyina and were joined by additional replacements from the 124th Cavalry and 613th Field Artillery. In spite of the name, they were really foot soldiers. The merger was called the Mars Task Force. Around Christmas of 1944 we went on to Bhamo and central Burma. As we proceeded south and neared Mandalay, the British decided we were no longer needed.

Our group was then split up and sent to Yunnan Province in China to train Chinese troops.

Words fail me when I try to describe my tour with the Marauders. Each soldier carried a three-day supply of C-rations, sometimes K-rations. Other supplies were parachuted in after a clearing was carved out and there was no danger of Japanese nearby. We had mules to haul our ammunition and weapons. In addition to the fierce battles, the harsh jungle conditions, the diseases of malaria, dysentery, typhus, and others, there was the constant fear of snipers.

The Marauders marched 600 or more miles through the hills and jungles of north Burma. They engaged in five major battles and 17 skirmishes. They made their mark in military history.

Sincerely,
Julius E. Rengel
Great Valley Basha - CBIVA

Franklin, IN

Dear Dr. Constein,

My husband, George, flew 67 trips across the Hump, piloting C-46s and C-47s from April 1942 until a December 31, 1943, crash. Following his military service, he was a traffic engineer for the state of Indiana for 38 years. He became an Alzheimer's victim, but I used to read the Hump Pilots Association Newsletters and books about the Hump to him. Until March 2001 he could still understand what I read to him. He died in his sleep Sunday morning, July 29, 2001.

He arrived in India in March 1943, first assigned to the 2nd Troop Carrier Squadron in Yangkai, China. After several months he was reassigned to the First Ferry Group at Mohanbari. If I'm not mistaken, that field was next door to where you were based at Chabua. He received a half dozen medals, including the Air Medal. He returned from overseas in May 1944.

He often talked about how from his plane en route to China he could spot Merrill's Marauders and their mule train on the Ledo Road. He did not know then, of course, that among the Marauders down below was my brother Willis Mead, nor that after the war Willis would marry George's younger sister Helen.

Like George in the air, Willis had a tough assignment on the ground. After fighting in the South Pacific, he volunteered for hazardous duty in another theater. It turned out to be the new theater of operations called the CBI. Fighting behind enemy lines in Burma, only 1300 of the original 3000 Marauders reached Myitkyina, the final objective.

Four days after George's memorial service at the Salem United Methodist Church and military burial, the Salem Leader *carried a tribute and a story about the brothers-in-law who served so well in that distant theater of war. My brother practiced law for 45 years, but his health was affected by his jungle experiences in Burma.*

Yours truly,
Pauline Reyman

P.S. We have a granddaughter Jessica Reyman who is performing for the second year with the Pennsylvania-based Re-Creation Troop at Veterans Hospitals throughout the US this year. We are very proud of her doing this.

Arcadia, CA

Dear Dr. Constein:

Yesterday I received the November, 2000, newsletter of AACS and saw your letters published there. I want to order your book.

My purpose in writing is to tell you that I flew in a C-46 over the Hump from your base, Chabua, India, to Kunming, China, on the night of May 17, 1945. We were a plane-load of troops seated in canvas-belted seats along each side of the cabin with barracks bags piled high down the center. You may have been my pilot. I recall we landed at 2 or 3 a.m. My MOS was 805 (Crypto), and I was assigned to Kunming Airbase. I stayed there until November 26 when I was flown back over the Hump in a C-54 to Panargarh, India, where my assignment continued until April 20, 1946. I was discharged on May 26.

Forty-nine years later I learned about the 19th Annual AACS Convention in San Diego. Since it was only a short drive from Arcadia, my wife and I attended the convention. Ever since then I have been trying to piece a few things together.

For instance, in the June '98 issue of our newsletter I read about the "Battle of Kunming." I remember that night well. I was working the swing shift. We were ordered to shut down all operations, draw a carbine and ammo and stand guard around the perimeter of our message center. The only action I experienced was being shot at going to and from our hostel and the airbase. American troops at that time were under the protection of the Chinese Army, and for about a week gunfire erupted from the Chinese Commie troops in the area.

I really enjoyed your book and will include it among my memoirs for my three children and seven grandchildren.

Best regards,
John R. Dawney
130th AACS Sqn.
Kunming

▶ The letters John referred to came about because Delight E. Breidegam, a friend of mine and member of the association, invited me to contribute them to the newsletter. I was able to help John locate Chabua and Penargarh on his map. He told me that Panargarh, the "East India Air Depot," was a wrecking yard for all aircraft being left behind in the CBI.

Alden, NY

Dear Dr. Carl:

I can't believe how parallel our lives have been—German Lutheran, choir singers, interest in music and the performing arts, Hump pilots. I graduated in 42-F in the Southeast Air Force training Command, instructed six or seven Basic Training classes at Greenville, Mississippi, then shipped over to Jorhat for 96 trips (like you) to China in C-87s. I came home for R&R, then (foolish boy) went back to become CO and Operations Officer at A5, Kiunglai in the Chengtu area. You may recall that was the west-end operation for B-29s. I stayed there until 1946, missing out on all the airline jobs.

I have a CBI video converted from 2000 feet of 8mm film I took over there. Let me know if you'd like to borrow it.

CBI friend,
Charles G. Koester

Chestertown, MD

Hi,

Your book brought back memories—the names of towns, the rest camp in Shillong, high in the Casi Hills. I enjoyed my stay because of the cool weather.

I was unfortunate to have fifteen bouts of malaria. They sent me to Karachi to be returned to the states. I recall sitting on the banks of the Indus River when a GI rushed up to tell us that President Roosevelt had died. We flew to Casablanca, arriving there the day the war in Europe ended. Then we continued on to the Azores, Newfoundland, and finally New York. I swore then I would never fly again. I haven't!

I was a S/Sgt Medic with the 2nd TC Squadron. When we arrived in the CBI we were sent to Yangkai, China. After a half year we were sent to Dinjan, India. That's all the flying I did over the Hump. Thank God; that was enough for me. Our assignment in Dinjan was to drop supplies to the infantry in Burma. That's when we started losing planes, mostly shot down. We were blessed by having good officers. The enlisted personnel were okay—a few bad apples but they didn't last long. Our squadron had thirteen planes. We lost 60 percent of our flying personnel in the first six months. Everything went wrong—being shot down, crashes on takeoffs and landings, and at times, as you wrote in your book, having a plane take off and never hear from the crew again.

By the way, after thirteen weeks of medical training when I first went in, I was sent to Olmstead Field, Middletown, PA, not far from where you live. There was no room for me in the barracks. I slept in a tent and nearly froze to death in that severe winter of '44.

Thanks again.

The best to you,
Harrison W. Vickers III

Reading, PA

Dear Carl,

My Army Air Corps group left for the CBI as replacements in early 1943. We arrived by ship in Bombay then flew to Dum Dum in Calcutta. We were assigned to Panagarh and later to Asensol, a few miles down the road. I was fortunate. Because of flight training at an airport in Reading five years earlier, my status in the CBI changed from general replacement to liaison and glider pilot. Here's how that came about.

Our designation was the 47th Repair Squadron. When the staff found out I was a certified pilot, they gave me a tool kit and assigned me to repair L-5s. I was like a tech rep, going from base to base for this work. I did this for seven months.

Then the 1st Air Commandos came to Asensol from Africa with their planes and gliders. They were a self-contained unit of nearly 600 men under British control. They had more than 200 planes—P-51s, B-25s, C-47s, L-5s, gliders, L-1s, and six R-4 Sikorsky helicopters. Our base, the Eastern India Air Base, was the largest in the area and therefore able to accommodate them. The Commandos used our runways for glider-snatching training.

One day I was called in by the head of the 1st Commando Group, Col. Philip Cochran. He asked me to join them. I was sent to Karachi for six weeks for glider training. Back at Panagarh I was handed an envelope detailing my status for a big mission called "Operation Thursday."

The date was March 5, 1944. I was at the controls of a CG4A glider, one of two to be snatched by a C-47 "Goony Bird" and towed to Broadway, a runway 150 miles behind enemy lines in Burma. After takeoff we followed standard procedure—climb for 15 minutes, make a hard left, climb again for 15 minutes, turn left at 4,000 feet, then gradually climb to 8,000 feet to clear the Chin Hills.

This was my first night glider flight into enemy territory. I was pilot and John was copilot. Our cargo was a 75mm Howitzer, ammunition, and three West African Chindits. There were no lights. Waiting for the connection, it seemed like hours went by. It was actually about 50 minutes. We got a call on the radio, giving us our final orders. Finally the hook-up came.

When we started we had light from the moon so we could see the tow plane and the glider on the right side. With luck, it would be okay like this. Two hours later the clouds grew thicker and the moon dimmer. An hour later we couldn't see the tow plane at all. John looked at me and said, "What now?" I told him to give me the altitude and airspeed every few minutes.

I heard a voice on the radio. "Captain Frank, is everything okay?"

"Yes," I answered the Chindit in the rear of the glider, "everything is all right," trying to hide my own concern. With changes in temperature and winds, there is a lot of creaking and cracking in a glider. I understood why my passengers were worried. Suddenly the running lights on the tow plane came on. John and I couldn't figure out why.

The next task was to look for a signal light on top of a bamboo pole, aimed upward. When we spotted it, we would be about 600 feet from the landing area. Finally we reached it and were released. We made a wide circle to the left, spotted the smudge pots on the ground outlining the landing area, and went down. After a few slight turns we were lined up. Between 50 and 25 feet I gave the warning of landing. I put her down left wheel first then straightened out for a solid landing. We exhaled a big sigh. On this big mission, 54 gliders were used, and 17 were lost.

During my time there I also flew L-1s and L-5s, mostly for liaison, but also for spotting, and supplying. Unfortunately for me, the Air Corps did away with flying sergeants. Had they not, I might have stayed in.

Sincerely,
Frank Wenrich

Colorado Springs, CO

Dear Dr. Constein,

My husband, Fred Carman, also flew the Hump in WWII—87 missions. He died in October 2000.

Please send three signed copies of your book. His children and I would like to have a written account of much of what he related to us, as I'm sure your experiences must have paralleled each others'.

Sincerely, in grief and pride,
Emely C. Carman

Alton, IL

Dr. Constein,

My assignment was flying cast iron pipe out of Dergaon for the Ledo Road. I didn't fly the high route as you did but was confined to the "First Ridge." I flew 88 trips across the Rock Pile.

I want to bring you up to date on the Hump wallas whose books I read. The author of It's Hanger-Flying Time, *writes of his early days of flying. He includes a takeoff incident in Misamari when one engine quit cold turkey. He had the presence of mind to unlock the tail wheel and exit the runway onto a taxiway. After they shut down the good engine, the crew heard a knock on the cargo door of Ole Dumbo. Col. Pratt, CO of the base, wanted to know what happened. Pratt was quite a guy. At a staff meeting after the January 6-7 storm when a dozen planes and crews were missing, he was asked how many planes his base lost.*

"None," he replied.

That got their attention. "How come?" they asked.

"Because I didn't send any out."

"Why not?" they persisted.

He answered, "When I was employed by the airlines, we didn't fly when the weathermen told us not to."

There should have been more COs like Col. Pratt.

I've heard and read a lot about the January 6 event. All I know is, I would not have cared for it. But flying through so many thunderstorms has taught me never again to be afraid of them on the ground.

Back to the engine failure. The cause of the failure was a bird nest in the air intake. I can vouch that that can happen. On a C-46 engine check at Dum Dum one day, we could not reach required power. We taxied back to maintenance. They wrote it off and we made a second attempt. The same thing happened. Then they found it—bird nest in the air intake. It had to have been built by the birds when we were being loaded. The AAC corrected the bird nest problem by putting air plugs in the air intake with long red streamers!

Ralph Piper's book Point of No Return *confirms the same problem. Ralph refers to another animal incident. He lived on a farm. One day he rented a Cub and flew home, landed in a field, parked, and started toward the house. The pet dog barked and carried on like mad. As soon as the dog heard his master's voice, he couldn't apologize enough. Ralph had been stationed at Tezpur and later Tezgaon, flying C-87s. He retired from Monsanto as their corporate pilot. He is deceased. As far as I know, Wiggs is still living.*

I had one brother who was in a tank destroyer outfit in the Battle of the Bulge, and another who was a navigator with thirty-five B-17 missions over Germany. They were my heroes.

Incidentally, this past Veterans Day I had a card from a lady at the church thanking me for having served in WWII. I told her the only other thanks I received was from Harry Truman when I received his official thanks and the "Ruptured Duck" lapel pin.

Regards,
William O. McDonald

New Smyrna Beach, FL

Dear Dr. Constein:

Your book will be an enjoyable stocking-stuffer for my husband for Christmas. He too had many interesting experiences over the

Hump, one of which was to fly Keenan Wynn, William Gargan and Paulette Goddard over that treacherous region.

We both read Tom Brokaw's two books about "The Greatest Generation" and agree that he could have at least mentioned you Hump pilots. I know there are others he has missed as well.

Very truly,
Jeanne M. Geho

Short Takes

■ Jack Goodman (Glasgow, KY): *I also flew out of Chabua—76 round-trips, 600 hours. Six of us who graduated in the class of 44-F from Altus, Oklahoma, get together every year.*

■ Kenneth G. Keisel (Pittsburgh, PA): *My Hump experience was 97 round-trips out of Chabua. After the war I became a corporate pilot. Now I read about flying instead of doing it.*

■ Bob Tyndall (Hillsdale, NJ): *My heartfelt thanks and appreciation go out to you and all other veterans of WWII for the wonderful job you did.*

■ Bud Bovard (Malvern, PA): *I too flew out of Chabua. I'm certain we held at 500-foot intervals over Kunming sometime. I trust you will explain in your book where the last fifty-five years have gone.*

■ Russell W. Selles (Tacoma, WA): *I consider my tour of duty in the CBI to be the most momentous period of my life.*

■ Bert Winder, (Middleton, DE): *I also flew 96 round- trips over the Rock Pile. Send me your book. AND DON'T FORGET TO SIGN IT.*

■ Ray Kuhlman, Procrastinator Emeritus (Kinston, NC): *It's been a long time, but this old Tezpur pilot remembers.*

■ Frank Johnson (Tampa, FL): *Send me a book. And keep your flying speed up.*

■ Dick Russell (Indianapolis, IN): *Your account of flying the Hump accurately describes my experience flying 87 round-trips out of Sookerating. God bless you for your efforts in keeping these memories alive.*

■ Carlene Grieshaber (Metarie, LA): *My husband was 19 when he made his 77 round-trips out of Mohanbari. I'm hoping he will enjoy your book as an extra little Christmas gift.*

■ Mary R. Holt (Carmi, IL): *My husband (deceased) flew the Hump. He retired from Pan Am as a 747 Captain. My children and grandchildren remember the glory days; your memoir may help them understand what went before.*

■ Ike Trumbore (Bethlehem, PA): *It was a pleasure hearing your talk at our CBIVA Basha dinner about flying the Hump. I drove the Ledo Road to Tingkaksaken, Burma. You flew those soft fluffy clouds, I drove through them. They were damp and cold.*

■ Tony Giaimo (Parsippany, NJ): *I was a C-47 pilot out of Sookerating, 1st Troop Carrier Sqdn, May '44 to April '45. I was pilot on two trips for Pat O Brian and Jinx Faulkenberg. I was in your town of Reading on Pearl Harbor Day.*

Hanover, NH

Dear Dr. Constein:

I was among the first group of navigators to go to the CBI after General Hap Arnold almost got lost flying from base to base over there. He said, "For God's sake, you need navigators if you are flying missions in this area with its high winds, monsoons, and treacherous mountains."

The Hump Pilot Association's membership roster includes the names of 78 navigators who served in the CBI, twenty-eight of whom were assigned to the ATC. Navigators were extremely useful in certain hazardous weather conditions that often developed over the region. I was stationed at Jorhat.

My wife and I attended the 50th reunion of the HPA in Kunming in 1999. It was a great time for reminiscing. It brought back both fond and tragic memories.

Sincerely,
Henry Hayden

▶There were no navigators aboard on my 96 round-trip Hump flights. I believe they did not fly on C-46 flights.

▶Other veterans who reported they paid return visits to the CBI are James Bolton of Tacna, AZ, and Carl Trick of Cowdrey, CO.

St. Petersburg, FL

Dear Carl,

Your story parallels the story of all of us who flew the Hump. I was stationed next door to you in Mohanbari from January 6, 1945, to the end of the war. Coming home by ship in December, I ran into storms on the North Atlantic, as you did.

What prompted me to write was a name on page 115 of your book—Bill Spatz. I wonder if it was the same Bill Spatz who was with me in flight training. My Bill Spatz's address was 455 Penn Avenue, Sinking Spring, PA. I lost track of him when we came overseas.

Best wishes,
Robert L. Moore

P.S. I too was in education—teacher, principal, school board member.

▶Bob had the right man. Bill died after a long illness traced to anoxemia he suffered when his oxygen masked failed on a C-46 Hump flight from China. I was able to put Bob in touch with Bill's sister, Pat Snyder.

Frederick, MD

Greetings Carl,

I enjoyed your book. Although we both served in the CBI, my military service was entirely different from yours.

I was 29 when I was drafted in May 1941 and sent to Fort Meade. At the time I was a CPA on the staff of Ernst and Ernst in Baltimore. I was put on hold until the Army received the special order for my shoes—size 5! I was assigned as office clerk and "go for" for a master sergeant. This was not for me; I applied for OCS and received a 2nd Lieutenant's commission, Quartermaster Corps in September 1942 to E Company of the newly-activated 478th QM Truck Regiment and served with this company (redesigned 3945thQM Truck Company) during my tour in the CBI.

In April 1943 I arrived in Ledo, India, via Bombay and Calcutta. While the Company was in Calcutta I ran convoys of trucks to Ledo for use by the Chinese. Then the third platoon, to which I was attached, was sent to Jorhat, India, one of the Assam Hump bases. My assignment was overseeing the loading of Hump cargo planes—ammunition, bombs, rations, and gasoline.

In January 1945 the whole Company was recalled to Ledo. I was assigned Battalion Investigating Officer and other duties. For the first time since Fort Meade, I was bored. But in September the Allies secured the crucial city and airfield of Myitkyina, Burma, and the Company was sent there. We moved to Waingma, Momanck, Bhamo, Pangkham, Kutkai, and Lashio, staying in each of these Burma stations from about two to seven weeks. At each stop we set up a ration distribution point in the forward area for American, Chinese, and British troops and Burmese civilian rations for those released by the Japanese. The British administered Civil Affairs in the forward area and exercised control over the natives Burmese. We also issued hay to the Chinese for the mules accompanying them.

While I was in Bhamo I had a particularly good experience. I was assigned to the first convoy over the Ledo Road. It was a thrill to parade through the Hump terminal city of Kunming on February 4, 1945—my 33rd birthday! We were flown back to Ledo the next day, my one and only flight over the famous Hump. I then rejoined my platoon in Bhamo.

I left for home by ship from Calcutta and arrived in Newport News, Virginia, in July. Before I was discharged I was ordered to report to the NY Procurement Office to audit contracts in New York, Philadelphia, and Baltimore—this in spite of an abundance of points for discharge. In November I was finally discharged and immediately rejoined Ernst and Ernst.

In retrospect, most of my military service was interesting. I rode an elephant, for example, before I rode in an airplane. If you flew supplies to Burma and were unloaded by Indian Labor Troops in green uniforms—well, that was my platoon.

I left E&E in 1950 and went with the General Accounting Office in Washington and later with the Army Audit Agency, retiring in 1974. I returned to Frederick and have remained single. Further: "The Deponent Sayeth Not."

Best wishes,
Jacob E. Engelbrecht

Columbia, SC

Dear Dr. Constein:

Thank you for calling me after my inquiry to 1st Books Library about purchasing Born to Fly the Hump *and to signing it for my father, Al Bienert. He will be 83 on May 8 and will be receiving the book as a surprise birthday gift. I know he will enjoy it immensely. This will probably call for a new Hump Pilots Association cap and a visit to the next reunion.*

Sincerely,
Ginger Webb

Devon, PA

Dear Carl (CBIVA buddy),

Two weeks after I enlisted in the National Guard in Philadelphia in 1941 I was nationalized into the Army Air Corps. For the next three years I was stationed in bases no more than 300 miles from home. At Ft. Dix, NJ (MacGuire AFB) I went into aircraft instrument training. The B-18s we had there resembled the DC-3s. By this time I was a staff sergeant and was able to have my bride in a cottage on the base. I was shipped to Blythe, CA, then to Great Bend, KS. There I got my first look at our sacred cow, the B-29. After several months I was sent to California for a sea voyage to India via Australia.

We entered the Indian Ocean, picked up a British escort, and ultimately landed in Bombay. The next leg on my journey was extremely uncomfortable—the long, dreary train trip to Calcutta. Our base was at Kharapur, an hour and a half to the north. We were short of everything, including B-29s. They finally arrived and were put to work, stripped down to fly gasoline and cargo over the Hump to our advanced base in China.

By now I was a T/Sgt in charge of 12 instrument men caring for 45 B-29s. We took turns flying the Hump to repair damage incurred during the Hump flights and bombing runs. Each trip required a stay of about two weeks.

I had ten trips over the Hump, each one an adventure. On one trip I experienced the scariest time of my life. What happened is that we developed severe vibrations in the elevator trim tabs. The farther we flew, the worse the vibrations became. The pilot gave orders to prepare to abandon ship. I already had on my parachute. We opened the bomb bay doors and I stood on the narrow walkway waiting for orders. My heart was pounding and my knees were knocking. The forest and valleys loomed below.

Then things quieted down and the pilot announced that the problem was solved temporarily. We arrived safely in China, but that plane did not make the mission.

Ultimately we left India by ship from Calcutta and sailed to Sydney, Australia, where we picked up Aussie troops, the toughest fighting men I have ever seen. We dropped them off in the Owens Mountains of New Guinea. Then we headed north toward our new destination, Tinian. En route toward the Marianas, for several days and nights we continued through the awesome might of US Navy, assembling for the Battle of the Coral Sea.

Tinian was a beautiful island, but small and partially destroyed. After six months the war was over and we headed for that magical place—home!

T/Sgt. John R. Page
68th Bomb Wing
20th Air Force

Anderson, SC

Dr. Constein,

I don't remember you, but that is not unusual as I met so many pilots while I was at Chabua. I was S/Sgt in charge of the parachute department from June'43 to May'45.

I flew with R. D. Smith in a C-47 to pick up bailouts and I also flew the Hump with Carl Rittenhouse. Carl lost his life on his fiftieth mission. As he left the east end of the runway at Chabua, the left engine caught on fire and burned the left wing off. No one who didn't fly it knows the danger of the Hump.

Nor its beauty. I went out one clear moon-lit morning about 4 a.m. with Carl. As we crossed the First Ridge, the sun was coming up in the east and the moon was setting in the west. It was a sight I will never forget.

As we remember,
John D. Nash

Altoona, PA

Carl,

I was happy to hear from Lou Porto that you joined the Great Valley Basha of the CBI Veterans Association. I have met so many interesting people and have made lasting friendships throughout the country through CBIVA. One of most interesting is Rusty Iliff.

Years ago my husband and I met Rusty at a national CBIVA reunion in Salt Lake City. We learned that he had sailed to India in 1942 on the same ship I had, the "Brazil." Our Brazil reunion group was having breakfast together the next morning and of course we invited Rusty. Well, he was the life of the party—a member of MENSA, the Poetry Club of America, and other organizations. We correspond several times a year.

In a letter last year he referred to a set of books called The Arabian Nights *by Richard F. Burton, translated from Arabic in 1886. He said it took him all winter to read it. I wrote to tell him that about a hundred years ago when I was in my teens—so I exaggerated by twenty years!—I had read the book* Royal Road to Romance *by Richard Halliburton. I recalled the observation in your memoir that Halliburton was stretching a bit when he told of swimming in the reflecting pool in front of the Taj Mahal. Of course you were right.*

I believe you learned from Wendall Phillips, national chaplain of CBIVA, that I was a wartime nurse who served in India. Before I relate my military experience, may I tell you the poignant story of another CBIVA friend, Jean Seidel, who had been a member of your Great Valley Basha there in Eastern Pennsylvania. She was a nurse in a jungle hospital in Burma and engaged to Robert T. Boody, a pilot there in the CBI. When her fiancé lost a leg in a plane crash, she nursed him back to health, but he broke the engagement because of his handicap. Later he wrote the book Food-Bomber Pilot: China-Burma-India, *dedicating it to Jean, "the girl who saved my life."*

I had joined the regular Army Nurse Corps before Pearl Harbor, intending to make it my career. On that fateful day, I was home on leave from Fort Sheridan, Illinois. I returned to "camp" as quickly as I could. One unit had already left for Iceland, then Europe. Another unit was sent to Alaska a few days later.

A word about Fort Sheridan, the beautiful old cavalry post on Lake Michigan. Pre-war army life there was pleasant—a sandy beach with good swimming, comfortable quarters, a lovely officers club with many social affairs. We were close to Chicago with all its night clubs. The city was friendly to soldiers. A short time after I returned from leave, a notice was posted asking for volunteers for foreign duty. Along with five friends, I signed up. Little did we realize our "destination unknown" would be India.

Our group of ninety-one nurses, the 159th Station Hospital Unit, was a tiny part of the six thousand troops aboard the USAT Brazil, to which I referred. The Brazil was the first troop ship to India. From Charleston, South Carolina, the voyage took sixty days to reach Karachi. En route we were given three days' leave in Capetown and Port Elizabeth, South Africa.

Our unit took over an old British cantonment in the Sind Desert eighteen miles from Karachi and nine miles from the airport. In spite of the long time the British were there, everything was very primitive. We lived two to a room in a six-room cement building. There was no plumbing. We carried water from one lonely water pipe stuck up out of the sand. At first we had no way to heat the water. Then we bought little stoves in Karachi. Good old Yankee ingenuity changed that. In three months our GIs provided showers in each room. In the hospital buildings themselves, in addition to tap water there were a few flush toilets.

In the hospital we had no battle casualties. Most of our patients had contracted tropical diseases or injuries from accidents. Often the diagnosis of a patient was FUO (fever of unknown origin) or NYD (not yet diagnosed). Each time a troopship arrived in Karachi, our patient census doubled or tripled. Most of the cases were dysentery.

There was a very nice officers club in Karachi, open every day. There was a dance every Saturday night. The British also had a nice club. We were allowed to wear "long frocks" there. Indian tailors could copy from magazine pictures and make our dresses. There were shops and restaurants in town and there was a very nice beach on the Arabian Sea. To me it was a "lovely war," and I still remember that time as my "season in the sun." Today Pakistan is a hotbed of dissension and strife as the neighbor of Afghanistan. In the news almost nightly, Karachi conjures up a place I knew so differently.

Just after Christmas 1944 my lovely life vanished. The unit known as "Merrill's Marauders" started their guerilla warfare in the dense Burma jungle. The 20th General Hospital, located near the Ledo Road in Ledo, needed thirty more nurses. None of us wanted to go. Our chief nurse chose fifteen from the original unit and fifteen from the unit that joined us after a year and changed us to the 181st General Hospital. Our CO told us at Christmastime that we would be going home in the summer. Now he promised the fifteen of us we would be with the first rotation group.

The 20th was much more primitive than our 181st near Karachi. Until our bashas were ready, we slept in a large ward. After six weeks we moved into the bashas, three to a room. No shower! There was, however, one solitary shower hut for all the nurses. I recall walking there wearing a raincoat during the monsoon season. There may have *been a restaurant in the village of Ledo, but I never saw one. Every once in a while we would walk to a native bazaar a few miles away.*

By this time the doctors had learned more about tropical diseases. We had many malaria cases, as well as typhus, dengue fever, malnutrition, and a terrible skin infection called jungle rot. The hospital also had a Chinese section. I was told we were not supposed to have to care for Chinese, but that our Commander, Dr. Isadore Ravdin (colonel, later general), had this section and operated on a lot of them who had been shot in the head. Apparently in combat they weren't able to follow orders to keep their heads down. Already a distinguished surgeon, after the war he became a brain surgery specialist.

I described some of this in a letter I wrote on March 8, 1944, to my hometown paper, The DePere (Wisconsin) Journal. *I ended by saying how eager I was after two years in the CBI to be sent "on foreign service to the USA."*

The last six months of my service were unpleasant. It was a happy day when fifteen of us who had been in India for longest found our names posted to return stateside on the first rotation order. We left Bombay in July of 1944.

I stayed in the Nurse Corps until October 1945, when I was scheduled to go to Japan. No way would I do that. I chose to resign. I married and with my husband traveled to many countries, ninety-six in all.

But never Japan.

I look forward to meeting you at a regional or national CBIVA reunion.

Sincerely,
Mary Harper

Belmont, NY

Dear Carl:

I enjoyed reading your book. Many of your experiences I relived vicariously.

I began my service in India at Karachi in May '44. From there, four other officers and I rode the rails to Calcutta via Lahore and Lucknow. We spent five miserable days on a hot, sweaty train. We expected to start fighting the enemy right away, but as you learned in the Army, it was hurry up and wait. From Camp Angus Replacement Depot I was detailed to Darjeeling for three months. Then I spent three more months at Rest Camp #5 at Shillong. Finally, in November I was assigned to Company B, 333rd Engineers. Our assignment was to build a road from Ledo, India, to Burma.

In April '45 Company B was sent to Myitkyina in north Burma to work for the Post Engineer—maintaining the road network, operating two water plants and the electrical generating plant, building a Coco-Cola bottling plant, operating a gravel pit, and other engineering jobs. While I was there I flew to Assam to visit my brother-in-law, Don Putnam, who flew C-46s to Kunming.

During my assignment in Burma I took many photos with my Argus A2F camera. Most were in black and white, which I could develop locally, but I also took some in color. I had to guess at my F-openings and timing, then I sent them off to Rochester for developing. I didn't see them until I came home in February '46.

Like you, I flew to the port of embarkation in Karachi in December '45. We returned to Seattle by ship. While I was in Milar I ran across Don, my brother-in-law, who was also on his way home, of course. He regaled me with stories of taking off from his field in Sookerating, immediately going on instruments, flying through turbulent Himalayan storms, finally touching down at Kunming, China, fifteen seconds after breaking out of the weather.

I have nothing but admiration for the men who flew the Hump.

Kindest regards,
George Bottoms

►I have wonderful memories of two weeks' R&R in Shillong, where George spent three months!

"Residential area of the north Burma city of Myitkyina after the siege. It was, as you described it in *Born to Fly the Hump*, all torn up." September 1944. (from George Bottoms)

Port Arthur, TX

Dear Carl:

You have a great memory. I'm trying to recall where I lived in Chabua. It was in the Headquarters area. Ours was in a direct line with the headquarters building.

My bunk was in the middle on the right-hand side. My roommates were McCabe, Halser, Larie, O'Tons, Hunnicut, Toomse, and Killingsworth. Killingsworth and I are the survivors. How sad. Most of us had transferred there from North Africa (300 hours—no credit). McCabe, Larie, and I had transferred fighters with the 5th Ferry Group in Dallas. All of us went through the Reno School. McCabe and Larie were in Cadet Class 42-K. My class was next—43-A. We *flew the early P-39s, P-51s, P-47s, and my specialty, the P-38s. We built up more than 1000 hours before going to North Africa.*

Back to the memories. Incidentally, we had a pet monkey in our basha we called "Memories." Names like Paoshan, Yunnanyi, Chanyi are coming back again.

About your novel Orchestra Left, Row T. *I really enjoyed the way you handled the plot and the ending. Have you read Art Sutton's book* Rainbow Around My Shoulders? *His phenomenon happened to me just the way he described it.*

Thanks again
Bud Imhoff

Cumru Township, PA

Dear Dr. Constein,

Your book Born to Fly the Hump *brought back many memories.*

I was Assistant Engineering Officer then Engineering Officer in charge of B-24 aircraft maintenance, 373rd squadron, 308th bomb group, stationed eight months in Chabua starting March 1943 and then twelve months in Luliang, China.

It was an unforgettable experience. I'll never forget the mud in Chabua during the monsoon season. One memory especially stands out—three Indians trying to get their truck, which was stuck in the mud, across the railroad tracks near Chabua while a train was coming, all this by the light of the moon.

After returning to the states I got a PhD, worked for ten years with G.E., and then came to Reading and worked twenty-five years for the Beryllium Corp and its successors.

Best regards,
John P. Denny

Encino, CA

Hi Carl,

I was delighted to read your memoir. Since I retired from my yacht brokerage at Marina del Rey in Los Angeles, I have been busy writing my autobiography, mainly for my grandchildren and great grandchildren. I'm not a golfer and would be bored to the gourd if I didn't have this writing to pursue. In fact, I'm afraid to finish the manuscript for fear I won't be able to find another subject.

My CBI story is varied. I was a member of the original group sent to India in May of 1942. I spent several months flying General Chennault's C-47 in China; starting a one-plane "China Express"; getting chased and shot at by Japs; saved by the AVG Flying Tigers; for several months living with the Flying Tigers and the CATF, their successors; getting bombed; meeting Vinegar Joe Stilwell; meeting Chiang Kai-shek and the Madame; visiting a dozen cities in China; going on a bombing mission with my C-47 over Saigon!

Then I flew fifty C-47 round- trips across the Hump, with such adventures as icing up, dumping out loads to maintain altitude, flying drop missions to supply rice to Wingate's Raiders behind Japanese lines in Burma, spending time in New Delhi arguing with the VIPs for more supplies, getting my rear end in a sling several times. (I have included in my manuscript tales of smuggling, pararescue, romance in Calcutta and Agra, and a few other stories barely fit to print.)

In your book you wrote about the storm of January 6-7, 1945, when you and other crews were put in extreme danger because of the CO's edict "The Hump is never closed." When I read that episode I was reminded of the time the Hump pilots at our base pilots went on strike, advising the CO that we would fly no more 55-gallon drums of gasoline until two Red Cross girls in Kunming were deprived of their personal sedans. Today this sounds like a major offense, doesn't it? But things were different in 1942-43. Our CO took fast action to see that the girls lost their wheels.

After 1,000 hours in the CBI, I returned to the States and instructed in the C-46 at Reno, where you and many newly-commissioned pilots received your transition training before going to the Hump. I became Flight Safety Officer, Accident Investigating

Officer, and wrote a C-46 Pilot Manual. Best of all, I met a lovely girl in Reno. We were married for forty years when she succumbed to Alzheimer's Disease. In 1980 her disease prompted me to coordinate a group of caregivers that created the Alzheimer's Association. I have been president of the L.A chapter and served on the board for twenty years. We are proud that we have been able to help millions of people cope with this terrifying illness, and we are working toward finding treatments and a cure.

A friend who is a retired screenplay writer was very excited about the stories I related in my first draft. He saw great possibilities for a screenplay portraying good guys, bad guys, adding spice and intrigue, perhaps even SNAFUs by VIPs.

Those were exciting times for all of us, and I encourage everyone to write about them. I would be delighted to hear from you, letter or E-mail. Congratulations again on a great read.

Cordially,
Jim Segel

Memphis, TN

Dear Dr. Constein:

I was the wife of Newton E. Hardin, a Hump pilot who flew out of Chabua, as you did. I am delighted that you have published a book that will acquaint others with the brave individuals such as yourself and my husband.

I want to order four books, three for my sons and a grandson as part of their Christmas, and one for myself.

Sincerely,
Louise A. Hardin

Rancho Mirage, CA

Dear Carl,

Congratulations on your memoir. My brother was also a CBI pilot. We never swapped war stories in the 40s, and until I read the history of the CBI I had no idea of what he had experienced flying the Hump.

After Art's death I discovered the four-volume history published by the Hump Pilots Association. Art's photograph and brief bio appear in the publication. I dedicated the volumes to the local library. Only 10 other libraries, including the Library of Congress, have the complete four-volume set. In its news release of 10 April 2000, the City of Rancho Mirage Public Library included the following tribute.

IN MEMORY OF A HUMP PILOT

"The Hump, the WWII air supply route to China from India, was established early in the war to keep China in the war. A unique limited edition four-volume collection records the exploits, the personal sacrifices, the hardships and accomplishments of those who served there.

"Arthur P. Wales (1917 - 1991) was one of them.

"Wales learned to fly small planes in 1939 at the Syracuse, New York, Airport. In 1941 he enlisted in the Army Air Corps Reserve and became an instructor in the pre-flight program at Syracuse University. He was called into active duty in 1944 and served in the China-Burma-India Theater of Operations.

"Art flew 48 supply missions over the Himalaya Mountains and was awarded a Medal of Meritorious Achievement. In 1988 he was decorated by the Republic of China for personal and professional achievements in aviation.

"A native of Troy, New York, Art returned to Syracuse after the war. He was employed by the L.C. Smith-Corona Typewriter Company, ultimately becoming vice-president of typewriter sales worldwide.

"More than twenty Hump pilots from the Coachella Valley attended the presentation and reception held by the library."

Carl, your publisher did a good job. Perhaps you have similar plans to present your book to the local library.

Cordially,
Michael C. Wales

Ordway, CO

Dear Carl,

Your book brought back a lot of WWII memories, some good, others not so good. I too was a C-46 driver. I flew 69 round-trip flights over the Ole Rockpile from Mohanbari next door to you in Chabua. I hope I won't put you to sleep with my account.

After I graduated from Ordway High I went to the Colorado Aggies at Ft. Collins to major in forestry. There were, I discovered, more forestry graduates than jobs, so I transferred to the University of New Mexico with a major in anthropology. When the Japanese hit Pearl Harbor I quit school at the end of the semester, came home, and in February went to Pueblo to take the exam for Aviation Cadets. I was told to go home and await orders.

In March I received not orders but 'Greetings from the President.' So, like you, I was drafted into the Army as a $21 a month private and sent to the "beautiful" state of Texas! I visited the draft board to explain but they ignored me. I spent the following three months in the Signal Corps. Finally, in January 1943, I received orders to report to the Aviation Cadet Attachment at Jefferson Barracks, St. Louis, for ground school courses in meteorology, navigation, theory of flight, aircraft engines, aircraft ID, and Morse Code. I also did a lot of marching on the parade ground. After three months I was sent to the Cadet Classification Center at Nashville. Of course this was backwards—I should have been classified before I took preflight.

I took Primary Flight Training in Jackson, TN, on the PT-19. I was glad I wasn't assigned the PT-17 Stearman, because it tended to ground-loop. I was then sent to Basic Flight Training at Gunter Field, Montgomery, Alabama, where I had a 19-year-old Englishman as instructor. We flew BT-13s. Then it was on to Napier Field, Dotham, Alabama, for Advanced Training on the AT-6. I graduated with the class of 43-D then went on to gunnery at Elgin Field, Florida. I sure did want to fly fighters, either Mustangs or Jugs, but the ATC needed pilots so many of us ended up in transports.

I was sent to Miami for C-47 training. After that, it seemed, the Army Air Corps didn't seem to know what to do with us. We were sent to Billy Mitchell Field, Milwaukee, where we did nothing but check the bulletin board every day for orders to be shipped out. Finally I was sent to Salt Lake City for C-46 training.

What we found out there was that the 46s had been grounded because of a rash of accidents, some of them resulting in fatalities. Again, they didn't know what to do with us. I put in for leave and came home to Ordway. At the end of the leave I took my wife back to Salt Lake City with me. We had a wonderful month together before I shipped out to training for transition training on the C-47 and C-46.

I was to become copilot of a five-man C-46 crew. We were sent to Romulus Airbase, Detroit, where we would wait for a C-46 to roll off the assembly line at the Curtiss-Wright factory in Buffalo, New York. In the meantime, the brass hated to see us sitting around doing nothing so they made us ferry pilots.

My first ferry mission was to fly a PT-26 from Ft. Erie, Canada, to Newark, New Jersey. That plane is like the PT-19 but it had a canopy and a heater, a Godsend to me on that cold December flight. Next I flew copilot on a B-24, factory-fresh from Ford's Willow Run plant to Fresno, California. We deadheaded in a B-17 to Tucson, picked up a B-24 J for ferrying to Lincoln, Nebraska, where we RON'd at the Junra Airbase just 25 miles form Ordway. I was able to spend one last night with my wife before being sent overseas.

We returned to our base at Romulus then deadheaded to Buffalo to pick up our brand-new C-46. We flew the new bird to Miami, picked up two C-46 engines and took off on an assigned heading. Bob Collard, the pilot, was given an envelope which he was not to open for thirty minutes.

He opened it and learned that our destination was Chabua, India. Our route was Puerto Rico; Georgetown, British Guiana; Belem and Natal, Brazil; Ascension Island; Accra, Ghana; Kano, Nigeria; El Fashir and Khartoum, Sudan; Aden, Arabia; Misarah Island (known as "Misery Island" because of the flies by the millions); Karachi and Agra, India; and finally Chabua, India. The following morning we were rerouted to Mohanbari, where we remained until we got the 650 hours needed to go home. Even then we had to fly until our orders were cut to go home. I knew of several guys who had reached their

"650" and then were killed in crashes prior to receiving their "going home" orders.

In addition to my ATC service, I was on temporary duty with the 2nd Troop Carrier Squadron flying C-47s from Dinjan then later Shingbwiyang. I flew 47 missions, mostly drop missions to troops behind the lines in northern Burma. I also flew cargo into Myitkyina and Tingkwaksakan, Burma. Once in a while we'd return to base with bullet holes in the plane, courtesy of Jap ground troops.

Carl, I didn't intend this to be a book. Hope I didn't bore you.

Best regards,
Ed Gregory

►I never met Ed. I regret to say that when I called him for permission to use this letter and the reprint that follows, his widow, Zenetta, informed me, sadly, that Ed had died the previous week. The reprint, adapted, is printed with permission of Frank J.Dutko, Gulf Breeze, Florida, editor of the DELTA EAGLE.

GOONEY BIRD MISSIONS OVER BURMA

By Ed Gregory

In July of 1944 I was sent on temporary duty from my base in Mohanbari to Dinjan, India, to fly C-47 air drop missions to allied troops behind Japanese lines in Burma. On this TDY I was attached to the 2nd Troop Carrier Squadron. When we dropped to US or Chinese troops, we supplied the "cargo kickers," but when we dropped to British-controlled troops, (Indians, Gurkhas, Aussies, Africans, British) the Brits furnished their own kickers. We dropped by parachute, except for rice and peanuts, which we dropped free-fall, packed in layers of burlap. It was amusing to watch the Chinese troops trying to catch those heavy bags.

Many of the drop zones were fair-sized clearings in the jungle, and it was easy to hit the target with our cargo. Sometimes we had to make drops to an Aircraft Early Warning DZ, a postage stamp atop a prominent hill. If there was any delay between the "drop" signal from the pilot and the action by the kickers, the cargo would end up in trees so tall that it was impossible to retrieve it. I'll bet there are a lot of fat monkeys around those ACEW stations.

In August our unit was moved to Shingbwiyang in the Burmese hills. It was cooler there, and I finally got rid of the prickly heat I had picked up in Dinjan. Near the base was a nice stream where we could swim when we weren't flying.

On one mission to an American unit near Mogaung we had to make passes over the DZ to drop the big load of cargo. As we pulled up after the fourth pass, a cargo kicker came running up to the cockpit. "They're shooting at us," he yelled. Landing back at our base, we found five bullet holes.

We were sitting ducks for marauding Japanese fighters (Zekes, Oscars, Tojos), for we had no fighter cover. We flew down on the deck to avoid being spotted. I was lucky and never did get jumped. However, on several flights I spotted Jap fighters flying high and to the north, presumably heading for ATC planes over the Hump. We saw a few Jap planes that had been shot down by our fighters.

When I began my TDY with the 2nd TCS, the allies controlled the important strategic field of Myitkyina, Burma, but the Japanese still controlled the city. We flew everything imaginable into Myitkyina—Gurkha troops, Jeeps, trailers, gasoline, oil and grease, 6x6 trucks, bombs, ammo, rifles, rations, an Allison engine, and airplane wingtips. On more than one flight we were ordered by the tower to hold our position because they were being strafed. We had to worry about being shelled by artillery and shot at by snipers as we took off and landed.

On August 21, after two missions out of Ledo, India, my TDY ended and I was flown back to Mohanbari. I had logged 45 missions and 126 combat flight hours. The flight surgeon thought we needed some R&R, so we got to spend a week in Calcutta, living it up at a British country club, enjoying the best meals we had on our entire tour in the CBI.

"Our basha at Mohnabari. We lived four men to a basha, double-deck bunks!! Seems as if I always got stuck in the upper bunk. It was hotter up there, especially at night." (Ed Gregory)

Schwenksville, PA

Dear Carl,

I was a senior at the University of Missouri when I enlisted in the Army Air Corps to become a pilot. I received my wings and commission in March 1944, was made a twin engine instructor for three months, then I was assigned to Rosencrans Field in St Joseph, Missouri, for transition to the C-46. In September I was assigned to fly the Hump out of Chabua, the base where you too were stationed.

My first Hump trip was a night flight as copilot. I had been given no orientation to the route to Kunming, the approach, or even what the pilot expected me to do. After I returned to Chabua, I went to the flight simulator and memorized the instrument approaches of ALL *the bases we were using in China.*

After checking out as first pilot, I was later made a check pilot and instructor for pilots newly arrived from the States. That was okay, except it was a bit awkward when I had to check out flight officers who were our former instructors in Primary Flight School back home. Most of them had many more flight hours than Aviation Cadet graduates like me. It was not an easy task.

To conserve fuel, the checkouts of pilots were performed on actual missions. In the spring of 1945 a C-46 crew bailed and made its way back to Chabua. Later their plane was found 60 miles from where they had bailed out. Apparently the C-46 had flown well on autopilot for that distance until it struck a mountain peak. I was asked to give the pilot a check ride to assess his flying skill.

I was assigned to perform this check on a flight to Bahmo, Burma. After less than an hour into the flight, this pilot became extremely emotionally upset. His unreasonable fear caused him to cry. I returned to Chabua, and he was hospitalized in the nearby 234th military hospital.

An investigation was held. It was determined that the bailout was unnecessary. The pilot apparently gave the order to bail out because of his inordinate fear of adverse weather conditions. It was determined that he could not discern the difference between the sound made by ice flying off the props and crashing into the fuselage and an engine cutting out. The pilot was taken off flying status and returned to the USA.

This traumatic experience, along with other experiences in the Hump operation, caused me to reflect about the field of study I would pursue after the war. I had been a chemistry-math major. When I returned to the University of Missouri for graduate study, the dean ruled that I did not qualify to switch to psychology. I persuaded him to admit me to the psychology program under academic probation. He agreed, and in 1949 I completed my doctorate in Counseling Psychology.

One last matter. I recall you referred in your memoir, Born to Fly the Hump, *to the base chaplain at Chabua, Captain Unger. Well, I had met Elinor in St. Joseph and returned there after I left Chabua. I learned that Chaplain Unger was living in the Midwest, and we were fortunate to have him assist in our wedding. Chaplain Unger became a career chaplain in the Air Force He has attended several conventions of the Hump Pilots Association.*

I remained in the Air Force Reserve for ten years. In my work as psychological consultant, I piloted my own plane to cities throughout the East.

Carl, let's get together early in 2002.

Best regards,
Lawrence D. Edmonson

Southampton, MA

Dr. Constein,

Hi. I enjoyed your book so much I sent my copy to a friend. Please send me another copy.

My career in aviation began in Buffalo, New York, in late summer, 1942. Two friends and I went there to seek our fortune in high-paying defense jobs. We stayed in Susan Monahan's rooming house for $3.00 a week, pretty much in line with my 63-cents-an-hour pay. We never found our fortune.

During that summer of '42 Selective Service induction hung over all of us. Our goal was to become fighter pilots. I applied for Aviation Cadets at the Springfield draft headquarters. I flunked the physical. But I did get into the Air Corps and was shipped to Turner Field, Albany, Georgia. From there I was sent on another train ride to Chanute Field, Illinois, for sheet metal school. The coach to which we were assigned was filled with an Alabama football team. Until they reached their destination, these great big guys sat while we stood.

After overseas training at Camp Luna, Las Vegas, I ended up in a hotel in Boca Raton, Florida. At 3 a.m. one morning we were loaded into a 6 by 6 truck and driven to Miami's 36th Street Airport. We were served an elegant breakfast, the last good meal I had in two and a half years. When we crossed the ramp I was shocked to see we were heading for a C-46, the same type as that pile of junk I had seen at the Curtiss factory in Buffalo.

The two Pratt & Whitney R2800 engines shook and rattled. We swayed and bounced. Some guys lost their breakfast. After what seemed forever, we were finally airborne. To this day I am proud of the fact that I didn't lose my breakfast. Our destination was Chabua, India.

Our basha was located in a large tea patch. There seemed to be no organization and no one in charge. Finally, I was told to report to the 10 by 20 ft shop named the Jing-Bao Shack. On my second night I was called for guard duty. The Burma jungle was just a few miles away. The night was pitch black, the jackals were howling, the rain was pouring down—and I was scared. Charlie Edwards, my new boss, persuaded the chief guard that my time would be better spent patching up airplanes, so that was the end of my guard duty.

Chabua was first supplied by C-87s, most of them lost when I arrived. The record showed: C-87 #3791, lost over Hump on 9 April, '43, never found, six dead; C-87 #3696, lost over Hump on 28 April, never found, five dead; C-87 #3669, lost over Hump on 7 May, never found, five dead.

Then C-46s were brought in. The first fatal crash on "my" C-46s occurred on 2 August, 1943. Number 2420, supposedly our safest plane, was fitted for passengers, among them the famous war correspondent and CBS television reporter after the war, Eric Severeid. All twenty-six persons aboard bailed out when the plane developed engine trouble. Only the copilot, Lt. Charles Felix, failed to make it. A search team reached the survivors in fourteen days, and it took ten days to walk the one hundred forty miles to Assam. There were four fatal accidents in August, resulting in twelve casualties. By the end of October seven more planes had crashed, with the loss of twenty-two crew, C-46 #2307 having been shot down over Ft. Hertz by five Zeros. Only the pilot, Lt. Thomas, survived. My friend Sgt. Albers, the radio operator, was a casualty on this flight.

In December I had a pleasant surprise. My brother, Bob, had just graduated from Cadets as navigator and was assigned to ferry a C-46 from the states to Mohanbari, a field just west of Chabua. An intentional ten-mile navigational error allowed Bob's plane to land in Chabua! I was delighted to see him. I entertained him by our hitch hiking to the typical Indian unkempt town of Dibrugarh.

By December, '43, Chabua had lost twenty-four C-46s, some because of the 46's tendency for engines to fail on takeoff. A directive from the Curtiss factory kept me busy installing immersion pumps inside the fuel tanks by cutting an access door in the underside of the wing, then cutting a hole on the fuel cell and bolting in the new pump.

Activity expanded rapidly at Chabua and we were suddenly evicted from our nice new barracks to make way for newly arriving officers. We were shunted off to a new tent city beyond the polo grounds. The four men who occupied a tent together were George Bottoms of Taraboro, NC, Ed Knauff of Harmony, PA, Vernon Connors of Skyland, NC, and myself.

When we arrived in June 1943, rumor had it that we would be rotated home in nine months. Soon that stretched to twelve months, then fifteen, etc. Our slogan was "Home Alive in '45." Soon that became "The Golden Gate in '48" and "The Bread Line in '49." There were other slogans, some amusing, some unprintable.

In April 1944 Connors and I managed to get leave to Darjeeling. En route we finally arrived at midnight at a railroad junction called Siliguri. Tired and hungry, four of us opted for a 45 rupee ($15) taxi ride to our destination rather than wait hours for a train. Our all-night treacherous ride up the mountain finally ended at the peak just as the sun rose on the Himalayan peak of Kanchenjunga, at 28,248 feet the world's third-highest mountain, 55 miles due north of Darjeeling. The memory of that sight will remain with me forever.

Back at the base, the spring-summer monsoon had arrived. Rain poured down day after day without letup. Our shoes were green with mold, and our clothes would rot away long before they were worn out. In spite of the weather, our planes continued to fly twenty-four hours a day. I don't know how the pilots stood it. The planes would disappear into the clouds at the end of the runway, the pilots would go on instruments, and three hours later they would drop out of the clouds and land at Kunming or another field in China. New pilots might fly a half dozen trips before they got a peek at the mountains.

September came and the monsoon ended. Our tent had rotted away and we were issued a new one. More C-46s kept coming from the states. (Total C-46 production was 3,330.) Curtiss-Wright could manufacture them as fast as we could smash them up.

Our chaplain at Chabua was Orville Unger, a popular fellow who relinquished his monthly liquor ration for the benefit of the parishioners who took communion. During the big battle for the strategic city of Myitkyina, Burma, he would volunteer as cargo kicker for dangerous C-47 missions to supply our troops behind enemy lines.

Not all the plane crashes at Chabua were caused by engine failure or weather. In January 1945 a Chinese pilot belly-landed his P-40 on our runway. When we asked him what went wrong with the landing gear, he replied, "Me forgot." January 6-7 was the worst day ever on the Hump—fifteen planes lost to weather.

After another R&R, this one to Shillong, the war over, it was time to go home. Connors and I did not admit it, but we were both afraid to fly home or even to the embarkation port of Karachi in those C-46s. Everyone secretly feared that after a long stint overseas, something might go wrong on the journey home.

Finally, the Florida coastline appeared late in the day. I recall seeing the underwater coral reefs between the Bahamas and Miami. I can still feel our DC-4's wheels scrunching down on the runway of the 36th Street Airport. I had made one long, exciting grand circle.

Best regards,
Ted Hendrick

▶Ted is the author of *Three years and Three Days: A Memoir of WWII.* You can write to him at 52 Cold Spring Road, Southampton, MA 01073.

Livingston, TX

Dear Sir:

I recently visited with our mutual friend George Wenrich. He gave me your memoir to read. I served more than two years in India, not as a pilot but as a ground officer. During that time most of my friends were pilots. I got to listen to stories of their flights and other experiences.

I think the Hump story would be of interest to my children and grandchildren, not to mention great grandchildren when they get a bit older. Please send me a copy of your book.

Sincerely,
Albert A. Rice

Phoenix, AZ

Dear Carl,

There is one record I believe I can lay claim to on my first tour of duty overseas: I may have been the most faithful, most prolific letter-writer in the CBI! Every day, beginning on September 13, 1944, and ending on May 31, 1945, I wrote to Mary, my bride, who was serving as a WAVE at the Long Beach, California, Naval Hospital. I estimate that I wrote about 150,000 words with my trusty Parker 51 in those nine months. Mary saved the letters, and after I returned to the states, Aunt Ethel graciously volunteered to type them for inclusion in a family book I called Till We Meet Again.

It will be no surprise to realize that the main content of the letters was a daily litany of my love for my wife, my longing to be home, my wish for an early end to the war. Included within the pages are accounts of my flights and my life on the ground in India. I wrote my first letters from Miami and Nashville.

My first assignment was to ferry a C-87 to India. The C-46 ferry crews shipped out in a hurry, but the four-engine guys like me just sat around and waited. After awhile everyone became restless. Finally our plane came off the line at Ford's Willow Run Aircraft Plant, and orders were cut for our crew to ferry C-87 #271 to India.

My good friend Dr. Fred Stone was pilot; I was copilot. We left Miami on September 28, 1944, and flew on to Porto Rico; Natal, Brazil; Ascension Island; Accra, Ghana; Kano, Nigeria; Kartoum, Egypt; Aden, Arab; Masira Island, Arabia; Karachi, India; Agra, India; Barrackpore, India; Misamari, India; Tezpur, India.

Beginning on September 28, our correspondence was censored, so I couldn't identify the base I was writing from. Nevertheless, I was able to tell Mary that it was beautiful passing over the clouds covering the Caribbean. We had been gone a week when we caused a bit of excitement in one of our landings. We landed too long and ran off the end into soft sand. When I opened the hatch, fire trucks and ambulances were waiting. It wasn't serious, but it took two "Cats" to pull us back onto the runway.

At that field and wherever we landed, I bought little gifts for the folks back home, like an alligator bag for Mom, a belt for Pa, silk stockings for Mary. Meanwhile, my Short Snorter was growing longer and longer.

The next leg of our flight was 15 hours from Natal, Brazil, to Africa.

Over East Africa we flew over herds of elephants, but we were too high to get good photos. I did take some good shots of African Pin-up Girls and sent them to my bride so she could see her competition. For two weeks I had had no mail. I was anxious to get to our destination so I could read letters from home and then get to work doing my bit to get the war over with.

When we arrived in India, I learned I'd have to wait a while longer to pick up mail because we were ordered to deliver our cargo to bases all over India. Our quarters there were far from comfortable—no showers nearby, no lights. The nearby villages were stinky and full of beggars and hawkers. I wasn't exactly clean myself. In one stretch of a week and a half I didn't get to change clothes once.

On October 14 we finally arrived at Tezpur, our permanent base. I fixed up my little quarters in the basha as well as I could and built a desk for myself. My main anxiety was not the flying I would soon be doing over the Hump but the fact that I still hadn't received mail from Mary.

After two aborted flights, I finally had my first Hump flight. The weather was good all the way, and China looked beautiful with its rice paddies everywhere. On a night flight a few days later we hit a row of thunderstorms but we were able to top them. It was a sight to see—lightning flashing at the tops of clouds and little streaks of static lightning flashing past my window. There above the clouds, the bright moon shining, the view was magnificent. After the moon set, it was as though we were flying in an ink bottle.

I had promised to write to Mary every day. I missed on October 30 because, as I told her the next day, I was lucky to make it back from a flight. The number 1 engine quit on that flight and the inverters went out. That meant only three engines, no instruments, and a full load. We were able to set up the plane without much loss of altitude. We just made it to China. We waited there three days for an engine change.

A week later I had another memorable flight. Cruising high, a thick cloud cover beneath us, we spied high Himalayan snow-capped peaks, their proud heads poking out through the clouds. When we reached our destination, the captain let down and pointed out a village and a monastery in the high valley. Can you imagine living on a mountainous site ten or twelve thousand feet above sea level? A little farther on, we landed and saw a typical sight—thousands of coolies working on the runway, making little stones out of big ones.

By November 10 I had had nine trips and 80 hours as copilot. I had a long way to go to reach the required 650 hours. A few days earlier I had my first Q.D. ride to check out as first pilot. Later I was sent to Gaya in the valley for ten days transition training. After I returned, I had a number of check rides. I did well in every respect except night landings. The problem of landing continued to plague me, particularly landing attitude. My strong motive in wanting to fly in the left seat was that copilots were getting only two flights a week. I'd never make it home by July 4, which is the date I was shooting for. By March, copilots were in greater demand than first pilots, so when I was told I would not be checked out as pilot on the C-87, I figured it all turned out for the best. Meanwhile, as an avid photographer, I took and developed many shots over the Hump and around the base and in town.

My log book carries a special entry for November 12, 1944. As we sat on the line at Tezpur, pre-flighting a trip to China with a load of thirty-five 55- gallon drums of gasoline as cargo, we heard a tremendous boom. Concussion waves shook our plane. Although we didn't see the plane itself, we knew a C-87 had crashed on takeoff and feared the worst. All crews awaiting takeoff were ordered to debark and await a visit from the Operations Officer. Major Meyers soon drove up in his Jeep. He reported there were no survivors in the crash. Crews were given the option of aborting their flights or taking off for China. We decided to go. When we returned to Tezpur, we attended a safety meeting, where it was thought that confusion in the cockpit may have been the cause of the accident since two instructor pilots had been assigned to the flight. I will never forget the emotions I experienced that day.

Christmas is the saddest day of all, overseas. I wrote to Mary, telling her I'd be seeing her at Christmas Eve church service, singing carols and praying I'd soon be home safe and sound. I pictured her opening the big box of surprises I sent her to make her Christmas as joyous as possible under the circumstances.

▶ Lt.Col. Speckman has a letter dated January 6, 1945 in his book. He was to fly that day but was pulled off. He flew the next day. It's puzzling that his letter to Mary did not mention what is acknowledged to be the worst two days of weather in Hump history. In fact, in presentations I make to aviation and historical groups about the Hump and the CBI, I assert that January 6-7, 1945, were probably the worst two days of weather flying in Air Force history. Speckman's hairiest Hump flight came on February 7, 1945.

On the flight of February 7 our whole route was covered by a solid overcast topping out at about 19,000 feet. In and out of the tops of clouds we were surprised to see twin-engine C-47s and C-46s even higher. Just before we were to arrive at our destination, we entered a dark, cumulonimbus thunderhead. We were taking on rime ice, so we decided to climb out of it. We got to 23,000 feet but couldn't top it. The turbulence and static were so severe we lost radio contact. For safety we turned on all our lights and plowed through as we descended for a range letdown. We broke out over the field and Bob put her in nicely. We didn't want to RON, so we persuaded Operations into letting us file a flight plan as a weather ship. We made it home at 0200 hours.

I had a number of other tough Hump flights, including one on March 7 when we were stacked up over the field in China for two hours. A week later I flew with Lt. Fred Stone, basha mate and pilot of the plane we had ferried here from the states. This was our first flight together since then. The weather was unusual, completely cloudless—just the opposite of a flight a week later when the early monsoon struck. When we hit the runway in China that day, huge pools of water splashed over the plane and slowed it down. When we got out, we saw the whole plane was covered by mud.

To balance the danger, there was unimaginable beauty. Hump pilots who survived are blessed to have observed the most beautiful scenes Mother Nature provides anywhere in the universe. Looking out ahead of the ship, seeing white billowy clouds extending for miles and miles, reaching so high you can barely see their tops—all this splendor really makes you feel awfully small...just a small piece of metal in the sky trying to stay in one piece against the most severe forces the same Mother Nature can throw at you.

Meanwhile, life on the ground was getting boring, this in spite of all the movies I saw, the photographs I took and developed, the magazines and books I read and sketches I drew, the many Link Trainer sessions I had, and of course the daily letters I wrote. I don't want to tell you how often I lost or misplaced my Parker 51. By April 30 I needed only 39 more hours to qualify to go home.

My final Hump flight came on May 10. Bill Blake was first pilot. I came to the plane fully loaded with my camera and my movie camera. Bill was sleepy so I flew the ship to China, let down, and landed. Bill flew the plane home so I could use up my remaining film. The weather back in Tezpur was the worst on the trip. We let down, made a low-approach instrument landing, pulled up into the regular pattern, then were forced to do a 360-degree turn to avoid a plane taxiing on the runway. We came screaming in low, scaring the daylights out of the crews parked in the warm-up circle. We missed one wingtip by about three feet. What a finale to my Hump flying. A sad postscript to this story is that my good friend Bill Blake never got home from the Hump. He was killed in a crash.

On May 20 I got my orders to go home. We were told that air traffic was closed for rotating CBI crews home and that troop ships were the only means home. But we hit it lucky—we were assigned to take a plane home, with a two-star general, no less, as one of the passengers. After fifty-eight hours total flying time, we reached US soil in Miami. I wired Mary and told her I was so happy I could jump for joy. I stayed in ATC's Battle Creek Hotel for a day, then traveled by Pullman to Jacksonville and, finally, Long Beach, California.

Best regards,
Roland E. Speckman

Shillington, PA

Dear Carl,

Your book started me thinking about my flying in the service so many years ago. In September of 1944, a month after you graduated from cadets, my class of 44 H and I got our wings at Altus, Oklahoma. Most of us were assigned to Sedalia Army Air Field in Central Missouri. Nearest town? Knobnoster, population 643. I learned to play snooker there.

Sedalia was a Troop Carrier Command base for C-47 transition. We were trained in formation flying, parachute drops, and towing gliders. On one flight when we were shooting landings we took along a paratrooper who needed some jumps. He asked me to check his backpack and static line. Luckily for him, I discovered that his static line was under the backpack. Had he jumped, without a check, he would not have made it.

Our training was interrupted when we were switched to your plane, the bigger, stronger C-46 Curtiss Commando. Then, during the big Battle of the Bulge came another interruption. We were assigned to fly infantrymen to air bases near their hometowns for leave, then a week later to pick them up for deployment overseas.

Pilots were a glut on the market at this time. After my classmates and I qualified on the C-46, we were shuffled around the country—Baer Field, Ft. Wayne, IN; Topeka, KS; Kellogg Field, Battle Creek, MI. VJ Day came while we were in Ft. Wayne.

Finally we reached New York's Fort Totten for overseas processing. In mid-October 1945, we left New York, deadheading on an ATC C-54. We made stops in Bermuda, the Azores, Lisbon, Rome, Marseilles, Athens. We were forced to spend the weekend in Athens because Turkey was holding elections and permitted no foreign flights in its airspace. The next stop was Habbaniyah, Iraq, for refueling. What a hot, miserable place that was!

Then it was on to the replacement depot in Karachi, a big important city in western India. After the war, the sub-continent was partitioned into India, East Pakistan, and West Pakistan. Later East Pakistan became Bangladesh and West Pakistan became simply Pakistan. As an involved neighbor of Afghanistan, the country of

Pakistan—and especially the huge city of Karachi—has been in the news lately. While I was in Karachi I met Dr. Russell Derr, a flight surgeon from Adamstown, who was on rotation back to the states.

We continued on to Calcutta then headed east for China. I clearly recall that flight deadheading over the Hump. Foremost in my memory is the majesty of the Himalaya Mountains. Second, to pass the time we played poker, and I drew the only royal flush I have ever seen. That stroke of good luck may have been meant to deceive, for a short time later an engine started missing and we returned to Calcutta for repairs. The next day we tried again and made it to Kunming. I was much impressed by the terrain. We finally flew on northeast to Shanghai.

Our mission there was to relieve pilots who were heading home. My first flight was as copilot in a C-46F, which had hydraulic props. All my prior C-46 flights were in the 46D, which had electric props. I was flying with a guy I had known in the Civilian Pilot Training Program in Reading. He asked whether I wanted to make the landing. I said sure and moved into the left seat. I was accustomed to retarding the throttles at flare out prior to touchdown. When I did that in this aircraft, the bottom fell out and I made the smoothest landing ever. Rather lucky than good!

A special assignment which came our way was to load navigation hardware from the bases in China and take them to Shanghai for shipment stateside for decommissioning. One such flight stands out. Allen Day and I delivered 55-gallon drums of gasoline to Kunming. As we reached our cruising altitude of 12,000 feet on the return flight, the plane did not reach cruising speed. We finally realized the cause: neither of us had pulled in the boarding ladder. We engaged the autopilot, trimmed the plane for 120 mph and went back to the cabin to pull in the ladder. We donned parachutes, tied ourselves to the airframe, opened the door and pulled in the ladder. We made it.

In July 1945 we were transferred to the west field in Peiping. We were there to support General Marshall and his staff in the ill-fated attempt to mediate the dispute between the Nationalists and the Communists. The place was overrun with American bird colonels and generals. I recall one flight in a C-47 with a bird colonel as copilot. We landed at a number of fields, and all was going well. Our next landing was on a dirt runway. As we neared the end of the run out, our wheels sank into the ground. I later learned that in order to extend the runway, the Chinese had filled in a creek! Reluctantly, we stayed overnight as guests of a Nationalist general. The next morning—voila! Our plane had been pulled from the muck during the night and was sitting high and dry. But that isn't quite the end of the story. I was shocked on takeoff when I requested gear up and it did not retract. The colonel had failed to pull the unlock handle!

My military career was coming to a close. In November I left Shanghai via troopship to Manila. The long two-week voyage to Seattle was followed by a long train trip to Baltimore. I was mustered out of the service at Ft. Meade, Maryland, on November 16.

Best regards,
Marvin K. Bortz

Crescent City, CA

Dear Carl,

I recently discovered the Hump Pilots Association and saw your name in the roster. My mind flashed back to Primary School in Uvalde, Texas, where we first met. Then it was on to Waco for Basic and Advanced together. The good old days, I'd say. After the Class of 44-G graduated, I was sent to Fort Worth for B-24 transition, to Lincoln, Nebraska, for crew assignment, to Boise, Idaho, for crew training, then a long train trip to Seattle, to Los Angeles, where my home was, a home I couldn't visit because I was confined to the train for the whole 36- hour layover! From there to Fort Totten, NewYork.

After 35 years in plastic manufacturing, Rachael and I now live in the far north of California, 20 miles from the Oregon border. Ours is a low-key life where the most important activity is fishing for salmon and steelhead in the Smith River, which runs through our back yard.

Back to New York. It was late May when we left Fort Totten on the ATC shuttle. Naturally, we thought we were going to Europe. After an hour's flight we opened our orders and discovered we were going to the CBI, your bailiwick. My crew was assigned to the 7th Bomb Group, 9th Squadron, based at Tezpur, India. The group had recently been assigned to haul gasoline to China—for the simple reason that there were no longer any enemy targets to bomb within range of the airplane. Our B-24s were modified by removing the machine guns and hanging three 400-gallon gas tanks on the bomb racks. With the armor plate still in place, it was a heavy plane to lift off the runway. The further danger was that on return trips, the tanks had to be tightly capped to prevent the gas vapors from escaping, for a spark from the radio could cause an explosion. That would be the end of one B-24.

The runway at Tezpur was 6,000 feet. The rule was if you didn't have 100 mph when you reached the tower, you chopped off the power. I will admit there were takeoffs when I thought we'd end up in the rice paddy. When we finally got airborne, we had to hold back pressure on the control column to keep the plane from mushing back into the ground.

The object of our missions was to drop off as much gasoline in China as possible. We drained the bomb bay tanks and all but 1100 gallons out of the main tanks. The 1100-gallon restriction was not at all popular with us B-24 types—for two reasons. The first was that the gas gauges on that airplane were notoriously inaccurate. The second reason was that the prevailing west wind could get out of hand, at times seriously cutting down ground speed. On one return we landed at Jorhat and, as nearly as we could tell, had only 100 gallons of fuel left. That's not much for four 1200 HO engines.

Bailing out was on our minds a lot. This was especially true after my eleventh trip, when the sky was cloudless going over or coming back.

The Himalayas were breathtaking, and at the same time, terrifying. The thought of having to walk out of the mountains, assuming you survived the bailout, was not a happy prospect.

The flight I will never forget took place the first week in August. Returning from China at about 9 p.m., we ran into a ton of weather, and I had my first experience with St. Elmo's Fire. The interior of the plane lit up with a sort of luminescent glow. I felt static electricity, a prickly feeling, where the oxygen mask did not cover my face. I suppose the St. Elmo's lasted about 10 minutes, but it seemed like hours.

We fought that weather for three hours—alternately rising then falling at 3,000 feet per minute, airspeed fluctuating wildly, the copilot and I struggling to keep the plane right-side-up. When we finally landed and I hit the sack, I slept around the clock. The next day we learned that we had flown down the center of a squall line, a series of mammoth thunder-storms.

On another interesting flight we ran into severe icing conditions and had to use full takeoff power to maintain 130 mph, which is not much above stalling speed. We finally made it over the First Ridge. The ice came off in big chunks, doing some damage to the vertical stabilizers.

When the war ended, we had a plane down in Kunming for an engine change. There was some fear that the Communists might steal it, so my crew was deadheaded over to guard it until the work was finished. They issued us Thompson submachine guns for guard duty. Fortunately for us, no one showed up.

I made half my 39 missions after the war. Additional gasoline was needed to fly the Brass and certain planes out of China. As I recall, I made my last trip on October 8, 1945. I should point out that my 39 trips were not round-trip flights. When flying a bomber, every takeoff and landing combination was recorded as a mission.

Since we were one of the newest crews in the squadron, we were the last to go home. To help pass the time we buddied up with a group of GIs who had an ice cream machine and a fund of a couple thousand dollars which had to be used before leaving India. They threw a big farewell dinner at a Chinese restaurant in Tezpur, and we did our best to help deplete their fund. Whatever unpleasant memories we may have of flying the Hump were washed away that night. A fitting end to my brief service in the CBI.

With best regards to an old friend,
Gus Forsman

Whitehall, PA

Dear Carl,

For a small town boy from St. Lawrence County, NY, I suppose my WWII experiences and travels were in many ways similar to those of the other sixteen million American soldier-citizens. Knowing my draft number would soon be called, I volunteered after the third semester of college.

After basic infantry training and telephone lineman school, I attended radio operator school and civilian barber school! Yes, orders said that I was to keep heads clean in my spare time overseas! I was transferred from the Infantry to the Air Transport Command. Radiomen were desperately needed for airlifting troops and war materiel all over the world.

My first duty was in the Ferry Command, flying to Iceland and on to Scotland or Ireland, then deadheading back and doing it all over again. Next I was assigned to Grove, England, a hospital and supply base. Soon after the invasion of France we were making two supply trips a day to the front, returning with the walking wounded and litter cases. At the front lines we landed our C-47s on steel mats laid down by the engineers. I'm sure many lives were saved by the prompt care they received.

In the early fall of 1944 we dropped paratroopers of the 82nd Airborne into France and Belgium. I was on one mission pulling a glider into Holland. After Paris was liberated, I moved on to LeBourget, the field where Lindberg landed on his historic flight to Paris.

Taking off in a C-47 after a supply mission to the front, we had power in only one engine and ended up too close to the Belgian border. We were shot down by ground fire and I spent 33 days in a German prison hospital area, I escaped in fog and snow. After running for three nights and hiding in the daytime, I was caught in a barn. Luckily, I stumbled onto the French Roman Catholic Underground, and in about a week I was back in France and American lines. The German doctors had done a good job patching me up.

Following interrogation in London, I was sent out of the theater—short tours in Athens, Rome, Naples, Tripoli, Cairo, Abadan (Iran). Finally, around Thanksgiving of 1944, I reached my new theater, the CBI, and delivered a silver C-47 over the Hump to my new permanent station, Chengkung, China. From there we delivered to various China bases the supplies flown over the Hump. I made 116 trips over those majestic Himalayas. In addition, we pulled gliders in the Burma campaign and kicked supplies from C-47s to the Marauders from low altitude. By the way, I should tell you that "Phil the Barber" was also busy cutting hair on the base.

I had a few scary flights. One that stands out happened around the middle of July 1945. On takeoff from China, the two C-46 pilots and I were bathed in hot, pink fluid as the plane sprung a major hydraulic leak. We were forced to land in enemy territory. After a rough belly-landing, I was still alive. The Japanese pulled me out of the crashed plane and took me to Shanghai by truck. I was a POW in the YMCA building in Shanghai until three days after the surrender. American MPs broke in the door to my dark cell. What a wonderful greeting! I had been mistreated. In addition, I had contracted amoebic dysentery and scrub typhus fever. After a short hospital stay, it was back to flying, this time in four-engine C-54s ferrying air crews to Calcutta on their way home.

Finally it was my turn. I worked as radio operator all the way home—across India, Africa, and the South Atlantic to the Azores, and on to Bermuda, and West Palm Beach, Florida, where I entered the hospital. It was November 1945. I was discharged later that month at Ft. Dix, New Jersey. It was a real education that Uncle Sam had provided!

Best regards,
Wendall A. Phillips

Danville, IL

Dear Carl,

Like you, I left Miami Beach in the fall of 1944 for India. The toughest part of the trip was the terrible six days we spent on the train traveling from Karachi to Calcutta. In that timeframe we had a day and a night in New Delhi. After a little time in Calcutta we boarded another train for Chabua, where you too were stationed.

I was a long distance telephone man. Our lines went from Calcutta to Chabua, with several repeater stations in between. In addition, we took care of communications on the pipelines as well. The pipeline supplied gasoline to Tingkwaksakan in the Burma jungle. It was from the tank farm there that your planes got their fuel. We also got to Myitkyina and, as the war ended, to Kunming.

At the Chabua base the Signal Corps had its own area. In your book you said you did not recall seeing movies on the base. Actually, I do remember seeing movies there, but there were no USO shows. Incidentally, I saw Tony Martin at the Red Cross in Calcutta. The story was that he had washed out of Cadets because he flew under a bridge!

I didn't get home until the first part of April 1945. But at least I didn't have to survive a long, tedious sea voyage on a troop ship. Eat your heart out, Carl—I came home on a C-54 on the Crescent Run. En route we had engine trouble and stopped in Rome for one night. I got a little taste of Roman night life.

Before I came home, the Brass was seeking volunteers to search for the remains of aircrews lost over the Hump. I never heard whether any were found.

I'll send you several photographs I took in Chabua and Shillong. I still have the negatives. Way back then I did my own photo work.

Well, I rambled on long enough. One memory leads to another.

Sincerely,
Bill Nasser

Control Tower at Chabua, "crossroads of Asia."
(Photo from Bill Nasser)

More Short Takes

■ Jo Dushais (Santa Barbara, CA): *My husband, Wally, flew the Hump at the same time you did, out of Kermitola, as I remember. I also flew at this time, so we are excited about your book.*

■ Howard Petersen (Seattle, WA): *I was in India when you were, and your story sounds much like mine, except that I later went to Search and Rescue in B-24s. We are having our annual reunion in Penscola in September.* ▶ Gail informed me Howard passed away on May 16, 2001.

■ Bill Fanning (Crescent, GA): *I was a T/Sgt radio operator. After thirty-one B-24 missions in the 8th Air Force in Europe, I was shipped to Jorhat and completed exactly the same number of Hump trips in C-109s and C-87s. Needless to say, a blessed man!*

■ Gertrude Baier (Waco, TX): *Did you know my husband, Butch? He retired from the service in 1968. A second marriage for both of us, we had a wonderful ten years together until his death in May 1999. He was a wonderful man. If you were a friend of his, you are my friend also.*

■ Jack Renney (Stockton, CA): *I too was a pilot at Chabua during the period from November 1944 through November 1945. Perhaps we flew together.* ▶ We did not have fixed crews and therefore I flew with many pilots. Fixed crews would have helped our esprit.

■ Mrs. Helen Wollak (Mt. Vernon, WA): *My husband flew 100 B-17s to the East coast and then ended his flying career flying C-54s over the Hump. Several times he had close calls, but the Lord spared him to be with me for 56 years. Thank you for your interest in this area of WWII.*

■ Bob Blake (Morro Bay, CA): *I will be interested in reading your exploits over the Rock Pile. This C-109 driver is still shaking.*

■ Arthur B. DeRousse (Swansea, IL): *I was a gunner with the 14th Air Force in 1944-45, stationed in Chungking, Suichwan, and Luliang. I too was disappointed that Tom Brokaw had nothing to say about the CBI.*

■ Stan Nelson (Wichita, KS): *A navigator, I arrived in Burma on 10-8-45. I had a few Hump flights in C-47s and C-46s. My experience was therefore limited...but still memorable.*

■ Eddie Rapp (Tehachapi, CA): *An electrical flight line specialist, I serviced C-47s and C-46s in Chanyi, China. I'm a member of the CBIVA, Bakersfield Basha.*

■ Jim Ross (Baltimore, MD): *Greetings from an old Reading resident. I worked for my uncle (Kagen's Sporting Goods), took Civilian Pilot Training (Albright College and the Reading Airport—1940), ate good candy (Zipf's), and had a little fun with girls (Pagoda). I flew C-109s and C-54s out of Tezpur. Total flight time, including Ferry Command—2,900 hours.*

■ Dick Ruhnke (Skokie, IL): *As flight engineer at Chabua from July 1943 to August 1945 I may have flown a trip or two with you. I had 44 Hump trips, some very interesting.*

■ Jim Salmon (Claremont, MN): *I was a radio mechanic with the 4th Combat Cargo Group. We closed up the north strip at Myitkyina and flew those C-46s to Kiangwan, near Shanghai. What ever happened to all those old, beat-up C-46s we left there on the tarmac?*

▶ I heard, and I believe it's accurate, that all abandoned C-46s were gutted.

Waddington, NY

Dear Carl,

I was with the 124th Cavalry Unit. We were scheduled for overseas duty, awaiting the transport ship with mules already on it. The ship was sunk off the coast of Australia before it got to our port of embarkation. Just like that, we all became MPs, first as the 116th in Karachi, India, then the 272nd when we were moved to Shanghai, and finally the 701st just before we left China.

In Shanghai, we soon learned about Chinese thieves. They stole our vehicles, salvaging the motors for their junks and other boats. To prevent this thievery, we posted guards outside the city—MPs, SPs (Navy Shore Patrol), Chinese policemen, and occasionally, a judo master. If the thieves tried to escape with one of our vehicles, we had Thompson machine guns at the ready.

One night the guard stopped a weapons carrier in the city and discovered it had been stolen. The SP and the Chinese cop put the thief in the back seat and headed toward jail. Trouble began when, for a very short time, the cop took his eyes off the thief. In that brief moment the villain somehow managed to load the 32-caliber pistol he had hidden in his baggy pants. He stuck the gun into the SP's back and, shouting furiously in Chinese, gestured for the driver to stop the car. The SP thought what he felt on his back was merely the thief's finger. He turned around to face him. In an instance the SP was dead, shot three times through the heart. The Chinese cop pulled out an old German Wauser, put it to the thief's head and pulled the trigger.

I spent 18 months in the CBI, no day sadder than this one.

Your CBI buddy,
Hiram Badlam

▶My first classification in the Army was MP, like Hiram's. I served for five months with the 722nd MP Battalion in Philadelphia and hated every minute of it. I escaped by becoming an Aviation Cadet.

▶Badlam also related this episode in the Fall 2001 issue of the China-Burma-India Veterans Association quarterly, *CBIVA SOUND-OFF*.

Ashburn, VA

Old friend Carl,

Talk about long ago! It was exactly 64 years ago—three years before Pearl Harbor, in fact—that we met. I was a sophomore at Kutztown State Teachers College when you enrolled as a freshman. Our paths didn't cross that often, but I clearly remember your performances in the operettas Robin Hood *and* The Firefly.

I was at Kutztown for an under-graduate degree before applying to law school. Of course war intervened; we all went our separate military ways. Shortly after graduating, I was inducted into the Army Air Corps in New Cumberland, PA. My dream of a specialty in photography came to naught; I was given the honorable assignment of Tech Supply Clerk at Ellington Field, Texas.

In the fall a dozen of us sad sacs who met the educational requirements for Aviation Cadet training were called in and advised to apply. I asked about a Photography Cadet program. The captain acknowledged there was a limited program by that name. He said if I didn't qualify for pilot training I would be considered for an alternate program. My spirits rose, for I didn't really want to be a pilot, and I didn't expect to pass the physical. But my "best laid plans" went awry. I passed! My application was stamped PILOT.

I had no idea you too had become a pilot. I discovered that, as you reported in your memoir Born to Fly the Hump, *when I spotted this familiar looking guy asleep on the floor of operations late one night at Kunming. I can imagine your chagrin when you were awakened out of a dream by a stinging kick to the sole of your foot and, 12,000 miles from home, by hearing some grizzled kook greeting you in our Berks County Pennsylvania Dutch! One for the books, at least for your book.*

I recall an episode in your book about a weirdo first pilot with whom you flew before you checked out for the left seat. I had a somewhat similar experience. Flying copilot out of our base at Mohanbari one night, I pulled the gear lever. Nothing happened. The landing gear remained down and locked. I was shocked when Lt. Lemon (we'll call him) turned to the departure heading and proceeded across the Hump! I asked why he didn't call a Mayday and land. He said he did not have a turnback on his record, and he wasn't going to get one tonight. He told me to shut the hell up.

Loaded, how high could we go with the gear down? At 10,000 feet I moved the blower control handles to high blower position. My God! Both engines went from a full roar to a complete silence. I shoved the handles for carburetor heat full on. Nothing. Then I shoved both blower handles back and forth several times. All of a sudden the engines cut back in with a roar, over-speeding. Quickly they returned to the proper RPM for climbing. What a nice roar that had been! After we landed, I pushed the tail wheel lock handle. It too wasn't working. The tower instructed us to cut the engines and leave the plane sit on the runway. I never saw Lt. Lemon again.

I had a second hairy flight a little later in Gaya in central India. I was there to check out as first pilot. We flew out to an auxiliary landing strip to shoot night landings. There was a high overcast. The only lights on the ground were smudge pots marking the strip. All of us, the student pilot and those of us observing, were having a hard time finding the horizon. We became so mesmerized we neglected to check the altimeter.

Our downwind leg in the traffic pattern was to be 1,000 feet altitude above the ground. The elevation of the field was 1,500 feet above sea level. On the downwind leg the altimeter should therefore read 2,500 feet. When the crew chief saw that the altimeter read 2,000 feet sea level, he yelled, "My God, you are going to fly this thing into the ground!" The instructor and the student pilot both hit the throttles and pulled the plane up in time to save six lives.

After the war I taught for one year in West Reading. Then I attended Boston University for my law degree. I was admitted to the bar just in time to be called to active duty with the 89th Troop Carrier Wing (Reserve) in Bedford, Massachusetts. We flew—you guessed it—C-46s. But my primary duty was judge advocate. I retired in 1969, after which I worked as an attorney in the real estate department of the Southern Railway.

The third time you and I got together was at your place in October. We still have a lot to talk about.

Warm regards,
George L. Wenrich

Fleetwood, PA

Dear Carl,

I enjoyed your book about your 96 round-trip trips over the Hump. I was a crew chief stationed at Yangkai, 75 miles north of Kunming, which I believe you said was your normal China destination. The mission of our 11th Bomb Squadron (14th Air Force) was sea sweeps along the China coast from Hong Kong to Wenchow and through the Formosa Straights—hitting bridges and rail yards, and strafing enemy troops. I also had about a dozen flights across the Hump.

In October 1944 a few of us B-26 crew chiefs shipped out of Barksdale AFB in Shreveport, Louisiana, a Martin Marauder training base. Imagine our shock when we landed at Yangkai and saw nothing but B-25s! This was unbelievable. I had never even sat in or preflighted a 25. We were there to replace crew chiefs about to be rotated back to the States. No way would they send us new-arrivals home. Well, the 11th had a great line/flight chief who familiarized us with the Mitchel in no time.

In July 1945 we were deadheaded to Fini, India, to ferry back B-26s as replacements for our worn-out B-25s. We checked out in the sleek new planes and flew them home over the Hump, stopping off in Myikyina because of bad weather over the Hump. We finally got back to Yangkai. I can't recall whether or not the squadron flew any combat missions with these B-26s. It seems to me we may have been on a mission to drop leaflets after a ceasefire was ordered.

In September 1945 the 11th Bomb Squadron was scheduled to be shipped home. Top brass decided that these 26s should be flown to Germany for use by our occupation forces. The planes had been sitting in their revetments for at least a month. They required considerable work to make them safe for the long trip.

After a week of whipping them into shape, we were ready to flight test them. Lt. Russell and I were cleared to the far end of the runway. After the plane on takeoff cleared the runway, we were to taxi back on the runway for our takeoff. As the plane taking off made his run, we saw immediately the guy was in trouble, trying desperately to get airborne. As he passed us, we knew he was not going to make it. He ran off the end of the runway, hit a huge hole, cartwheeled tail over nose, and finally came to a stop. The plane burst into flames. We killed our engines, jumped out, and ran toward the crash. One crew member was crawling from the plane. I reached him and pulled him farther. He was badly burned but conscious. I remember trying to comfort him, assuring him he'd be okay.

Fred Garner, crew chief, died in the hospital in Kunming before I left Yangkai. I don't recall whether the pilot survived the crash. A few years ago Marty Oxenburg from Elkins Park, PA, searched the internet for the name Garner *in Boaz, Alabama. (Marty's role had been to get the crash victims to the hospital.) He found Fred's wife, Adelle, since remarried, and called her. For both of them, it was an emotional telephone call, he said. Adelle immediately called me. She thanked me repeatedly for filling her in on details which the War*

Department and the chaplain did not reveal to her. I still cannot believe that this chaplain never returned Adelle's calls.

The day after the crash Lt. Russell and I completed the flight test on the B-26 we were to ferry to Germany. Two days later we left Yangkai for good. Lt. Kelly was our navigator. I was lucky to have a competent crew, for we had engine problems approaching Abadan, Persia, and flew through some lousy weather crossing the Mediterranean Sea from Cairo to Naples.

In 1997 I had a letter from Ken Daniels, an engineer/gunner friend, who reported that after two years and 51 missions, he was told he would be engineer on a B-26 to be ferried to the States by way of Europe.

They were not told, he said, to fly only as far as Germany. The B-25, not the B-26, was his plane, so he and the pilots spent a week transitioning into the three 26s that were there. Suddenly, he wrote, they were ordered to burn them. *He refused. He was spared a court martial only because a fellow engineer torched the planes for him.*

Ken and I certainly had different recollections of the fate of the B-26s over there. I believe now we were both right. What probably happened is that the original order to deliver the planes to Germany was rescinded because of all the planes and crews lost in crashes on missions out of Yangkai as well as losses over the Hump and en route to Germany.

At any rate, our crew made it. We were flown to Paris, where we were split up and left to wrangle our own way home. I finally got to England, then set sail from Southampton aboard the HMS Stalker aircraft carrier. I arrived in Newport News, Virginia, a couple days before Christmas.

I feel honored to have served with the historic 11th Bomb Squadron. It was activated at Kelly Field, Texas, on June 26, 1917, as the 11th Aero Squadron. It served in World War One. George McManus, creator of the "Jiggs" comic strip enjoyed so much by us old-timers, was a member of the unit.

Let's get together for lunch. I'd like to tell you about the big rat invasion. Meanwhile, have fun putting together your new book.

See you soon,
Jesse Reifsnyder

▶Jesse and I are natives of the eastern Pennsylvania town of Fleetwood, the only two, we believe who served in the CBI. The name *Fleetwood* is well-known in automotive history because of the superior quality of bodies produced by the Fleetwood Metal Auto Body Company. In the company's honor, General Motors named its flagship Cadillac *The Fleetwood.*

The Eleventh Bombardment Squadron (M)

PART 2

CRASHES, BAILOUTS, CLOSE CALLS

Mission Viejo, CA

Dr. Constein,

A man with your record of flying the Hump would find the book The Aluminum Trail *most interesting. It is no longer available for purchase or library loan, but you may borrow my copy if you wish. I enclose a copy of page 48, which records our bailout and capture.*

Charles Montagna

7 November 1943 C-46 #5171 SOOKERATING DEAD: 1

CREW: Pilot - F/O Joseph E. Parris, T-185561

Copilot - 1st Lt. Paul E. Almond, O-494774

Navigator - 2nd Lt. James S. Johnson, O-800125

Crew Chief - Charles T. Montagna, 32434947

Radio Operator - William J. Flynn, 32422879

This ATC aircraft was en route from Kunming, China, to Chabua, India. It was reported as missing in flight when the ETA was up. A Jap broadcast was heard to state that American airmen had bailed out due to engine trouble over Japanese-occupied territory in Burma. It stated that two airmen had been turned over to the Japs by some Burmese natives. Another broadcast stated that two other airmen were brought into the civil internment camp at Maymyo and locked in a small cell. They were Cpl. Mantagna and Cpl. Flynn. The story told by Cpl. Charles Montagna states that the crew bailed out and were captured. He and Flynn were brought into Maymyo and the other three were taken to Rangoon. That is the last they saw of them. The treatment was very bad. They did manual labor, and five prisoners were locked into a small cell. The cell was about fifteen feet square and no sunlight. Sanitary conditions were bad, the food poor, and they slept on bare boards.

A letter dated 29 May 1945 states: Parris, Johnson, Flynn and Montagna were rescued from the POW Camp. 1st Lt. Paul E. Almond died Prisoner of War.

▶Quinn, Chick Marrs, *The Aluminum Trail,* Sequin Press, 1989

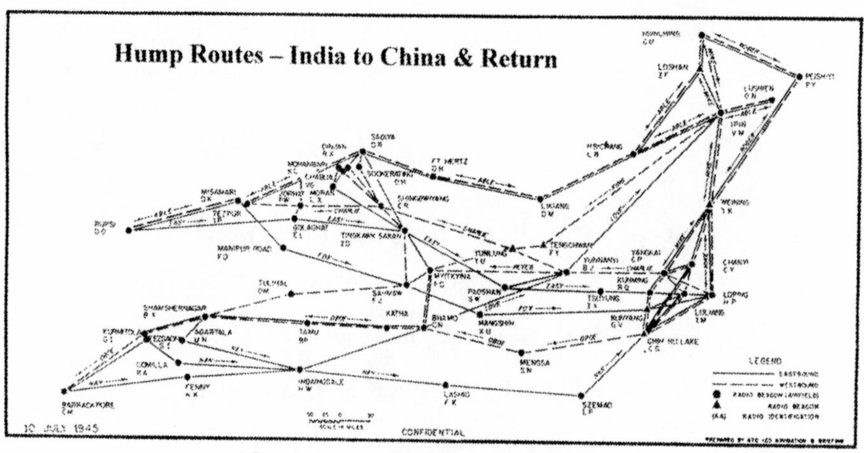

(Courtesy of Wendall Phillips)

Owensboro, KY

Dear Carl:

I congratulate you on your vivid description of flying the Hump. I too flew through that gigantic storm of January 6, 1945. According to my log, I left Mohanbari early in the morning of January 5, manifested to Tsuyung, China. On this flight I was to check out the pilot, whose name was Robinson, as C-46 captain. The next three hours were filled with terrifying moments of fear, doubt, and frightening concern for survival.

I don't recall exactly when the problem started, but we began taking on a thick load of wing ice and also carburetor ice. We could not maintain our assigned altitude of 16,500 struggling to stay at 15,500. For two solid hours we pulled emergency power on those Pratt and Whitney R2800 engines. We had such heavy ice that if we tried to climb, the plane would burble for a stall. We lost radio contact and radio navigation and made a correction for the strong south wind, hoping it was enough to keep us away from the Himalayas high peaks.

We finally flew into a clear hole near over the lake east of Mt. Tali and near Yunnanyi. We circled in this hole to dissipate the ice. We regained radio contact and proceeded to IX southwest of Kunming with a load of gasoline for a convoy that was stalled on the Ledo Road.

After the plane was offloaded, mechanics checked the engines and discovered a dead magneto on one engine. We were there several days waiting for maintenance to come from Kunming to replace the mag. We finally returned to Mohanbari on December 9, not entirely aware of the extent and severity of the storm. Everyone was shocked to see us, for after we had not returned on the 6th, we were reported as missing in action. Pretty lucky, I'd say.

Carburetor ice was a problem not just when you flew through severe cumulonimbus build-ups but whenever you were on instruments, which was most of the time. It gave us all anxious moments. The chief pilot came up with an experiment for the check pilots to try. We were each assigned a different carburetor heat setting to apply before we entered the clouds on our descent into the Assam Valley as we returned to our base in India.

My first experiment came in a night flight. I was given a partial setting to be applied when we entered the top of the overcast at 15,000 feet over Mohanbari. Both engines quit! I was flying the right seat as check pilot. I told the pilot to make a standard procedure turn and I would try to restart the engines. I failed and called the tower, declaring a Mayday to warn the planes holding in the stack below for their turn to land. I tried carburetor alcohol but this didn't work either. I then pulled both mixture controls into "idle cutoff", shutting down the engines, and let the props windmill. When we got below 5,000 feet I made a desperation move. I held my breath and shoved the mixture control levers into "full rich" to backfire the engines through the carburetors. My fear was causing an engine fire. Amen!

The engines started and we had no further trouble. Had they not, I would have ordered a bailout at 3,000 feet.

The upshot of all this was that I took some good-natured ribbing about my Mayday. But I learned one thing. From then on I went back to the carburetor heat procedure I had always used before—full heat when you enter the weather.

That's enough war stories for now. Thought you might be interested in my adventure during the big storm of January 6 as well as every C-46 Hump pilot's vexing dilemma of applying carburetor heat.

Sincerely,
Kenneth G. Jolly

►I recall endless meetings of pilots in the Chabua officers club called by the chief pilot to discuss carburetor ice. There was never a consensus. Like Ken, I was inclined to go for full heat before entering the weather rather than opting to try to break out the ice after it had formed.

C-47 (Douglas DC-3)

C-87, C-109 (B-24 converted for cargo)

C-54 (Douglas DC-4)

C-46 (Curtiss Commando)

Hughson, CA

Dear Carl:

I too was an ATC pilot in the CBI, perhaps the first to be stationed in China. You were stationed in Chabua on the India side of the Hump, I was stationed at mile-high Chengkung on the China side. Our squadron had twenty C-47s and C-46s. And by the way, our mutual friend Wendall Phillips from Whitehall, Pennsylvania, was a radio operator at Chengkung. I'm sure you know he is the national chaplain of the CBI Veterans Association. And I believe Tom Masano from your city of Reading was also at our base.

My year in China was marked by two memorable flights, one near the beginning, one near the end. The story starts in November of 1944. After graduating from Aviation Cadet training, I found myself in Nashville, in a pool of pilots awaiting overseas orders. One night I was ordered to report to a nearby airplane factory to familiarize myself with the C-47 another pilot and I were ordered to ferry to China. I'd had only one flight in a 47, and that was as second copilot accumulating time for monthly flight pay. Bailey had a little time in the 47 and he had more total flight time than I did, so he was assigned the left seat and I was to be copilot.

Bright and early the next morning, Bailey and I crawled into the brand-new C-47 as it sat on the floor of the factory. We took our seats in the cockpit and went over the checklist and examined the instruments and controls. Suddenly we were chased out of the factory because the Army Air Corps had not yet signed the papers.

Finally the plane was released and we overcame the first hurdle—taxiing the thing to the end of the runway. We realized there were many things we didn't know about this plane, so before taking off we took our time learning what we could. The tower called. "You are blocking traffic. What is your problem?" I looked back and saw 15 or 16 planes behind us, including one belonging to a two-star general, in line for takeoff. Bailey waved goodbye to his wife and two young children on the tarmac and pushed the throttles. A tear rolled down his cheek as he said, "I'll never see them again."

The C-47, the Douglass DC-3, has a history as the world's most stable, dependable airliner, so we had no trouble flying it to Miami.

But as we approached the field, we had to figure out how to lower the landing gear. Thus began a very close relationship between Bailey and me. On the long flight to China, I developed a lot of respect for him and his "quiet confidence" in life as well as in flying.

We finally arrived at our destination, Chengkung, in southwest China, twenty miles south of the big base of Kunming. Our mission was to deliver war supplies that had been flown to China from India over the Hump. We flew long missions to Chinese Army forward units. In that first month alone I logged 180 combat hours.

The first memorable flight I referred to in the first paragraph of this letter is one I didn't take! Late one night I was awakened by the CQ to prepare for our fourth mission. Before I was dressed the CQ returned and told me to go back to bed. I was being replaced as copilot so a new man could learn the route. It was to be Bailey's final flight. Returning to Chengkung after delivering its load to Sian, (famous now because of the terracotta soldiers discovered there) where the plane crashed on takeoff. All were killed. Crashes occurred so often in the CBI, and I was so busy trying to stay alive that Bailey's death did not hit me hard at the time. But later I couldn't get him and his young family out of my mind.

Like all of us young Americans, I learned a lot in China. I observed unbelievable cruelty among the people—punishment for minor thievery by being hoisted to a horizontal bar by a rope tied to thumbs, beatings by teakwood boards, a woman beaten to death with a heavy truck spring, pigs forced to lie still while being transported, heavy threads through their eyelids then tied to the floor of the trailer, Chinese troops in the back of our C-46s trying to push each other out the cargo door. I was born on an Iowa farm, so the pig episode hit me hard.

Still, we admired the Chinese peasants for the hard work they did with their hands—building roads, bridges, and runways, leveling mountains, plowing fields, loading and unloading our planes. They did this on two cans of rice a day, everyone wearing, even in winter, the standard blue thin cotton pants and coats and flimsy shoes made of rice straw.

The weather was our main enemy in flight. But the problem we discussed most of the time was not the weather but the food. The menu never changed—for breakfast, pancakes with weevily flour and tropical margarine, sugar and coffee; for all other meals, two small pieces of water buffalo, three potatoes with skins, greens, and rolls with the ever-present weevils.

Through the grapevine we learned that an infantry unit at the recently recaptured base of Myitkyina, Burma, had a big supply of food. The unit had been in action a long time and fresh eggs, which we had but they didn't, would be a real treat for them. Our squadron collected enough money to purchase 1,500 very expensive eggs. The problem was, how do we get a fragile cargo of two large straw baskets with 750 loose eggs from south China over the Hump to Burma in a C-46? We hired the coolies who had delivered the eggs to accompany us, and at the first sign of bad weather to pick up the baskets to cushion the shock. They did a great job. We landed with the eggs still unscrambled!

I was appointed pilot and negotiator. We arrived at the mess hall at 5 a.m. The first sergeant salivated over the eggs but offered only "beef willy" and canned milk in exchange. Part of my crew snooped around and reported the warehouse was filled with food. I asked to see the CO.

"Are you sure these eggs are fresh?" the colonel asked.

I assured him they were. "Sergeant," he ordered, "I want you to serve every man in this outfit two eggs sunnyside up. And I want you to give this man anything he wants."

We returned to Chengkung with a heavily loaded C-46. We were heroes.

Now let me relate the other memorable flight. On our way home from delivering cargo to a base up north, we were cruising, as we often did, above a solid overcast. Ahead we saw a line of bubbly, dense clouds indicating a front. I recall thinking I had made the right decision—go through the storm rather than around it. Go around it and we consume precious fuel and risk flying into high Himalayan peaks to the west.

I became less sure of my decision when hard rain and extreme turbulence bounced us around like a rubber duck in a bathtub. Extreme static cut off our radio communication. Without additional power we were climbing at 2,500 feet per minute. We throttled back, lowered the landing gear and flaps. To no avail. At first I wasn't particularly worried, for both Donnally, my copilot, and I had flown through many storms before. But we had never reached so high an altitude. At 30,000 feet I ordered the radioman to prepare to bail out, but while he was in the cargo compartment struggling to open the cargo door, I rescinded the order. There was no way we could get safely to the ground with chutes in air this turbulent.

St. Elmo's Fire made the cockpit weird. Rain hit the windshield and sparkling bits of static electricity fell on us as though it came through the windshield. Sparks built up on the ends of the windshield wipers like wet snow. The blades of the props became flame throwers. Even though we had on winter sheepskin jackets and oxygen masks, we felt the hair all over our body standing on end.

Suddenly there was a deafening bang. We had been struck by lightening. The radio operator was knocked to the floor. The copilot frantically pointed to the instrument panel. We were descending so fast the gauges were maximum down, the engines so cold they registered almost no oil pressure. Both of us were working furiously, retracting the flaps and landing gear, coaxing some power from those ice cold engines. I was worried about pushing the power on too fast. My biggest worry was our falling altitude. We were down to 11,000 feet in an area where the route minimum was 13,500.

I had to make a decision—hit the mountains or lose the engines. I pushed the throttles further. It turned out to be the right choice. We held at 11,000 and broke out into a beautiful morning, the sun rising over the mountains. We continued home with no more difficulty.

This flight changed my outlook on life, and I have shared it with my beloved grandchildren. I felt that God spared me because he had a purpose for me. At times I've wrestled with what that purpose was. I come back, always, to "doing whatever I can for my family and others."

After 106 missions I returned home to Iowa then moved to California. Life has been good—happily married, children and grandchildren, teaching career in agriculture. But the memory of my friend Bailey's death continued to haunt me. I tried often to get in touch with his widow and his children. I called government agencies in Oklahoma, where I believed his widow lived. I was unsuccessful. I took a different approach. I called the office of my Congressman, Representative Gary Condit. I spoke with the aide in charge of veterans affairs and learned that the last survivor's benefit check was sent to a woman in Lake Charles, Louisiana, in November 1998. I wrote to her and sure enough, four days later she called me. It was Bailey's daughter, the little girl who had waved goodbye there in Nashville so many years ago. We talked for two hours.

A week later I received a call from Bailey's granddaughter in Austin, Texas. She thanked me over and over again, calling me her angel and her grandfather's best friend. It was a moving experience.

Carl, in the CBI you were stationed in India, in the west, and I was stationed in China, in the east. As civilians, our locations are reversed. You are now in Pennsylvania, in the east, and I am in California, in the west. Regardless of that, the Himalaya Mountains and the CBI Theatre have forged a bond between us. My best regards to you.

Sincerely,
Raymond M. Rodgers

Los Altos, CA

Dear Carl,

I just finished reading your book about history's first airlift. It brought back memories of my experiences in the CBI and on the Hump, and also of your hometown of Fleetwood, Pennsylvania.

After the war I was a troubleshooter for a refrigeration company out of Syracuse, New York. When the Fleetwood Auto Body was sold to Fisher Body, the company began manufacturing refrigerated cases for meats and groceries. I'm sure you remember this. I went to Fleetwood many times to pick up cases by truck and take them to our plant for resale and installation.

The rest of your book is almost a copy of my life in the CBI, except that your flights were all Hump flights. I had 28 round-trip flights on the Hump itself, and the rest were combat missions delivering precious supplies to troops fighting behind the lines in Burma. My base was Shingbwiyang, Burma, where we lived in tents a mile from the field. I lost five of my buddies from my tent.

Even though I had only one takeoff and one landing in a C-46, I was made First Pilot of our 2nd Troop Carrier Squadron. Like you I suffered hydraulic failures, carburetor and wing ice, and mechanical failures on many flights. On my first flight to Kunming, I made such a lousy landing, frankly, that my young copilot refused to fly home with me. I had my radio operator fly copilot, and we made it okay.

The flight I remember most clearly took place on February 15, 1945. My crew and I were assigned a C-47 mission to drop twenty-five 200- pound bags of mule feed to Merrill's Marauders fighting behind Japanese lines in Burma. On board were Jay Frey, copilot, Jimmy Law, radio operator, and five quartermaster "cargo kickers." We had been warned by Intelligence before we left Shingbwiyang, that ground fire on Hill 369 might be intense.

I received the code of the day and took off, a small sack of silver rupees by my side, the money to be used to buy our way out of the jungle if we were forced to bail out. When we arrived at our destination, I spotted the code laid out on the ground in cloth strips and made a run over our markers at 500 feet. Suddenly, it felt as though a ton of bricks hit us. We had been hit on the right side by ground fire that tore into the tail, elevators, and ailerons. Fortunately, none of the crew were injured, and the engines were not hit. We were now over Japanese lines, too low to bail out.

I ordered Jay to have the cargo men kick out the mule feed and run to the rear of the plane. It worked! The nose of the plane lifted and we were able to climb to 3,000 feet. Then I ordered the kickers to move to the center of the plane and we were able to maintain our altitude. By gunning either engine, I was able to steer the plane. We headed west, away from the enemy.

I called the nearest field, a British base at Bhamo, Burma. They were in the middle of bulldozing the runway after a Japanese bombing attack. I called a Mayday and told them I had to land. I pulled back on the throttles and had the kickers come forward. As I approached touchdown, Jay gave the signal for the kickers to run to the back of the plane. The tail came down and we landed safely.

A British colonel came out in a jeep to congratulate us and invited us to lunch, the happiest meal I had in the CBI. We had survived and were deadheaded to our squadron at Shingbwiyang. It was only one of my 149 combat missions.

Please excuse the poor handwriting and misspelling. At my age writing is even more difficult than it used to be.

Your CBI buddy,
Ryan H. Dawdy

▶ *The Distinguished Flying Cross Society* recently printed Ryan's close call in its magazine under the title *A Near-Disaster Over Hill 369.*

Ryan Dawdy with his son and grandson at the Castle Airbase in Modesto, California. The plane is a C-46 Curtiss Commando. (his photo)

Phoenix, AZ

Dear Carl,

What a pleasant surprise to read the notice in the Hump Pilots Association's Newsletter about your WWII memoir. I really enjoyed the book. I remember that we had been together in Advanced Training at Waco, on temporary duty at San Angelo, transition training at Reno, then assigned to Chabua on the orders of 29 October 1944. Enclosed are copies of some of the assignment orders, including the order that sent you, me, Peterson, Fettaleh, and Bird from Chabua to Mitykyina on ten days detached service for the purpose of familiarizing a C-47 squadron of newly-arrived service pilots with the lower route to China. Remember how scary that was?

I believe I was billeted in the basha next to yours in the tea plantation at Chabua. My friend Don Downie may have been in your basha.

Talking about scary flights, the scariest I had, as you said in your book you did, was in the storm of January 6-7, 1945. I was still copilot then and hadn't had much actual instrument time. Downie was the pilot.

Our C-46 was a plane that had seen its best days. Like many I flew, the wing de-icer boots had been damaged and removed. I can't recall the cargo, but I seem to remember it was too bulky to throw out if we needed to. We weren't overly concerned about the trip, for many planes were landing on their return from China. Pilots we talked to reported rime ice but rather light winds. China, they said, was wide open.

We took off in the dark and immediately flew into a solid overcast. Nothing unusual about that. But after we crossed the First Ridge and climbed to our cruising altitude, turbulence picked up tremendously. The heater didn't work. I remember how cold I was. As we flew over Burma we were tossed about violently. Ice built up on the wings and on the hub of the props. To maintain altitude, we applied more and more power. Propeller ice released by the alcohol de-icers sounded like bullets as it hit the fuselage. It took both Downie and me on the control column to maintain a fairly level attitude.

As we got over China, my biggest fear was that we might be off course. The wind normally blew out of the west at about 70 mph. I don't know why, but I had the feeling the wind was out of the south. The problem was, the storm affected the radio stations along the route, our only means of navigation. All we heard was static. The radio compass needle spun constantly. Other planes must have had the same problem, a few of them calling Maydays, reporting that they were preparing to bail out. After tuning in to all radio stations we thought we were near, Downie got through to one fifty miles to the north of our course. Normally the needle would point north, just off our left wingtip. But it pointed south! We had been blown north of this beacon, somewhere among the high mountain peaks beyond ATC's most northerly route!

Downie called the tower for permission to land. We were told the field was below minimums. Perhaps 50 miles north of our route, we made a huge correction into the south and continued on to our destination in China. I recall we were wringing wet even though the cockpit was cold and the outside temperature was minus 20.

We flew on in ice and turbulence to our destination, Kunming. The field was reporting CAVU. How could that be? we wondered. Nearly over the field we broke out into the clear, a searchlight shining brightly like a welcoming lighthouse. We had made it!

Certainly we won't have to go back into this stuff tonight and return to Chabua, we thought. Well, someone in authority finally gave orders to close the Hump, but not until we were airborne and on our way home, out of radio range.

I am forever thankful that Lt. Don Downie was my pilot on that long flight that dark night. It was his skill and experience that kept us from ending up in the high Himalayas to the north, where most of the lost planes and crews are resting. Estimates of losses vary. I believe in your book you said 15. Even now, it was probably the worst weather the Air Force has ever flown in. The luck of the Irish.

Good luck in your tennis.

Warm regards,
Bill Hanahan

▶Captain Henry and I made an earlier round-trip flight in that memorable storm of January 6. If, in fact, we were among those Don and Bill asked for a weather report after we landed in Chabua, they would not have heard from us, "Light winds, light ice, China wide open." Like Bill, I am eternally grateful to the 1st pilot that day, Captain Henry. I feel I owe my life to him for his skill, for his professionalism in trusting the instruments, and for his openness in discussing decisions with me. Sadly and unfairly, a month or two later Captain Henry took off on a clear day and, mysteriously, he and his crew never returned.

Mullica Hill, NJ

Dear Carl,

I received your letter a few days ago and look forward to meeting you soon, perhaps at the CBIVA regional convention in Reading in June.

I enjoyed your book. My job in the CBI was Crew Chief, mainly on B-24s and B-25s. I was in Burma and India from March 1944 through November 1945. Life in the jungle was a bit rugged and boring. But there was one episode that wasn't at all boring. What happened is this.

It all began on March 19, 1945, when Air Jungle Rescue of the 10th Air Force received word that an ATC C-46 en route to Kunming, China, had gone down over the Hump because of heavy icing. The crew bailed out near Shingbwiyang in the heart of the north Burma jungle. The following day a Naga tribesman walked into the base at Shingbwiyang and handed the startled staff a note from the plane's radio operator, and the search and rescue mission was on. The Naga led a search party to the badly injured radio operator.

The next day a Naga chief came to the base. By gestures, he was able to communicate that he knew the location of the crash and of the other crew members. The base staff offered him money and gifts if he would occupy the front seat of a PT-19 Fairchild trainer to show the pilot the location of the crash. After two hours of searching, the pilot, Captain James L. Green, gave up and headed back to Shingbwiyang. The single-engine plane developed engine trouble and Green was forced to put down in the densest jungle in the world. He crashed just five miles from the airstrip. Unfortunately, the plane was not equipped with a radio so Green could not report his position. The C-46 crew was more fortunate. A ground search party found them and returned them to Shingbwiyang.

When Green was declared overdue, a C-47 was sent out. After a thorough search, the crew returned to the base. As they approached for a landing, they spotted the wreckage practically in the traffic pattern of their field. The next morning a team headed by Lt. William Diebold left to rescue Green and the Naga chief, if they were alive. Guided by an L-5 pilot giving radio directions, the rescuers slashed their way through the rugged jungle, arriving a day and a half later. They found Green under the plane, barely alive. His pants, wallet, and watch were missing, apparently stolen by Nagas who had found their chief dead. The Nagas were reputed to be headhunters, but they had not molested Green. Following undergrowth which had been trampled, the team discovered the chief's body in a shallow grave.

Captain Jim Lamberts, base flight surgeon, accompanied the team. He found Green delirious. He had suffered a concussion, a broken pelvis, a broken jaw, deep facial cuts, and internal injuries. Lamberts faced a dilemma—unless Green was evacuated he would die from infection and internal bleeding, but if he were moved, splinters from his broken pelvis might puncture his internal organs. Lamberts asked Diebold, the team leader, whether it would be possible to clear a site for an L-5 to land and pick Green up. Diebold shook his head. It would, he said, take a couple hundred men weeks to hew out a 1500-foot strip. What they needed, Dr. Lamberts said, was a skyhook.

The word struck a chord with Lt. Diebold. "My God," he said, "Air Rescue at Myitkyina has one," as he ran to his radio and called them.

Carl, here's where I fit into this helicopter story. First, a little background. The YR-4 Sikorsky helicopter was originally delivered to the Army Air Corp in May 1942. Its first use in the CBI was in April 1944 when Lt. Cater Harman rescued three British soldiers and an American pilot whose L-1 liaison plane had been shot down behind enemy lines in Burma. Lt. Harman later made several more rescues. When he was rotated back to the States, the YR was put into storage because no one else was checked out in it.

Then in January of 1945 a B-25 crashed in the jungle of Burma. General Hap Arnold got personally involved and ordered that a new YR-4 be disassembled and flown from Wright Field, Columbus, Ohio, to Burma in a C-54, together with two helicopter pilots and maintenance crew. As crew chief, I volunteered my crew and myself to reassemble the ship. In twenty-three hours she was ready to fly. However, it wasn't needed for this mission because the crew had walked out on its own. Later in the month an enlisted man in a mountain weather station shot himself in a hand. In a dangerous maneuver, the helicopter crew was able to evacuate him. The stateside helicopter group was ordered to remain in Burma a month to train pilots in the use of the YR-4. Unfortunately, the chopper was so underpowered that only a lightweight could pilot it. The officer chosen was Lt. Raymond F. Murdock.

Now back to the story of Captain Green's evacuation from the wreckage of his . Murdock took off first in an L-5 to survey the crash site from the air. He advised the ground crew where the landing pad should be carved out of the jungle. The flight surgeon, Captain Lamberts, said the rescue had to be made within a week. Lt. Michael Pecorare of the Combat Engineers led a group of engineers and base personnel to the site. They felled trees and dynamited tons of dirt to reduce an 18-degree slope to five degrees. Meanwhile, the story spread throughout the CBI and many volunteers arrived to relieve the exhausted workers. Using picks, shovels, and axes, they finished the pad on April 3. The surface of the "Airstrip of Pecorare the Greek" was deemed hard enough to accept the helicopter.

The following day, the elation of Pecorare's troops dropped when fog suddenly rolled in. But by 10 o'clock the fog lifted and Lt. Murdock took off from Myitkyina and headed for the landing pad. He had only 36 hours in the chopper and had never attempted a landing in such a tight spot in such dangerous conditions. On the first landing attempt, a downdraft put him beneath the ledge of the pad. He made the correction on the second try, facing the slope. The tail rotor blades nipped tree leaves as he descended but fortunately did no damage. He put her down in a hard landing. So far so good.

Murdock instructed the men to hold the chopper in place. After Green was placed in the passenger area, Murdock started the engine, whipped up the rotors to maximum power and signaled for the men to let go. The chopper rose four feet off the pad and stayed there. He pointed the YR-4 downward off the pad to get forward motion, gave her full power and blasted clear of the trees. Prayers turned to cheers as the anxious men watched. Soon the tiny dot disappeared and landed at Shingbwiyang.

The story doesn't end there. After dropping off his injured passenger, Murdock took off for Myitkyina, where he and the chopper were based. The YR-4 had had it. The engine sputtered and Murdock made an emergency landing on the Ledo Road. He called Air Jungle Rescue, and I was flown to the scene. Murdock and I took a short test flight. We determined this YR-4 was no longer air worthy. My crew and I brought a truck sixty miles up the Ledo Road from Myitkyina to disassemble the chopper and haul it back to its final resting place.

Every GI has a story to tell. This is mine.

Best regards,
Walter L. Carre

Ontario, CA

Dear Mr. Constein:

I have read your book Born to Fly the Hump *and I want to thank you for writing your story. Little is known, recorded, or documented about the China-India-Burma Theatre. My brother, 2nd Lt. Harvey Bos, flew the Hump around the same time you did. He was dedicated to our country. In a letter he wrote to our grandmother just before he was declared "Missing in Action," he wrote, "I got through flying school because I figured I had a job to do." He did that duty and paid the ultimate price, his life. He was only twenty-four and had been married only eight months.*

For fifty-five years my family was told my brother was declared "nonrecoverable." We knew little about the details of his death. Not knowing what happened to him left a black cloud over my life and affected me deeply. I had many nightmares and sleepless nights wondering what really happened to him. About two years ago my daughter decided to research his death in an effort to bring some sort of closure. After countless requests for information and many closed doors, she was finally able to have his IDPF files sent to me. A document in the file stated that my brother's plane and the remains of three crew members had been found. The remains were recovered unidentified and buried as unknowns in the Kunming, China, cemetery on 28 November 1945. The document went on to say that the Unknowns were exhumed, renumbered, and placed in the Remains Depot in Shanghai. The document contained a recommendation that further research be made to determine identities.

As fate would have it, the recommendation was never pursued. The document completely contradicted the facts that had been given to my family. This newly uncovered information would send us on a long search for the truth. I want to share with you the events that followed.

Our foremost quest was to find someone who flew with him and could give us information. First my daughter searched the internet—to no avail. Next she wrote our government officials for help. We got lots of feedback from senators and congressmen. One senator in particular, Senator Diane Feinstein, gave us her full support. Together with her chief-of-staff, Mark Kadesh, she spent many hours assisting us in our search for the facts. My daughter then decided to take our story to the media. It was through the media that we were to meet many wonderful people. We received calls from well-wishers who wanted to see us succeed.

One of the pilots we met is Mr. J. V. Vinyard of Amarillo, Texas. He flew the same route on the same night my brother's plane went down. In fact, there was only a one-hour difference in their departure times from their base in Sookerating, India. Mr. Vinyard kindly wrote a thorough, thoughtful letter to my daughter explaining what my brother probably experienced the night he died. Although reading the details was rough on me, his letter became a source of great comfort.

►This was the famous storm of 6-7 January 1945, the worst weather in Hump history. I flew to China and back earlier that day. Fifteen planes and crews were lost, most of them blown to the high Himalayan peaks to the north by 125- to 150-mile-per-hour winds blowing out of the south rather than the rather benign 75 mph winds normally blowing out of the west.

►Because Vinyard's letter has meant so much to Mrs. De Fouw, and because it is so descriptive of that storm and the entire Hump operation, I include it here verbatim.

"Dear Mrs. Apodaca:

"Thank you for the information you sent me on the search for your uncle 2nd Lt. Harvey Bos. I must commend you for the dedication you have shown in pursuing your request for information. A lesser person would have given up in frustration a long time ago.

"Please excuse me for not answering sooner. I just returned on June 30 (2000) from a visit to McChord AFB, Tacoma, WA, where the US Air Force Mobility Command recognized the Hump operation of World War II by placing "Flying the Hump" nose art on one of their C-17s. It was a great honor for us to have them do this. About 85 Hump members and guests attended the dedication ceremony.

"I am sorry for the loss of your uncle, as I am sorry for all those who did not return from the Hump. I was also stationed at Sookerating—from August 1944 through February 1945. There is a possibility I knew him and may even have flown with him, but I cannot recall him at this late date.

"You said you did not even know his group or squadron. In the Air Transport Command we did not operate in groups or squadrons as most of the Air Forces did. Our bases were identified as "base units." At Sookerating we were the 1337th Army Air Base Unit (AABU). The Air Transport Command was a worldwide command with bases all over the world. The AABU system was the way the Command kept track of where each base was. Sookerating was the farthest northeast base in the Assam Valley.

"At Sookerating we flew on a rotating basis. There were no permanent crew assignments. The normal crew for a Hump mission was pilot, copilot, and radio operator. On occasion the crew also included a flight engineer. Separate flying assignment lists existed for pilots, copilots, and radio operators. Flight assignments were made by chance.

"After return from a flight, each crew member went to the bottom of the list. The three at the top of the list made up the crew for the next flight. At that point each person on the list would move up one notch. Normally the number of people on each list was not the same. If the copilot list was the shortest, then pilots on that list would move to the top faster, thereby flying more often than first pilots did. This normally resulted in assignments of crew members who had not met before.

"The length of each list would vary dependent upon how fast copilots qualified to be first pilots and how fast older pilots were rotated home after their mission requirements were completed. Pilots would rotate home after flying 650 hours over the Hump, unless they volunteered to stay an extra three months, which very few of them did.

"As I told your mother, the night of January 6, 1945, was probably the worst weather night that occurred during the entire Hump operation. I also flew that night. There was little hint of the severity of the weather at the time we checked in at Operations to prepare for our flight. Returning pilots told me it was pretty bad over the Hump at the time, but to me most times it was pretty bad. So I gave it little thought.

"I took off about an hour before your uncle's flight did. Climb-out was northeast to Sadiya, a homing station (navigational facility) located about 22 miles northeast of Sookerating. We were required to climb to 10,000 MSL (mean sea level) over Sadiya before proceeding southbound on course. This was required because our base was too close to the first ridge of the Hump to proceed directly on course after takeoff.

"We did not enter the overcast until after we had turned southbound for the next homer, Shingbwiyang, Burma, our first en route checkpoint, about 100 miles away. As we neared our cruising altitude of 14,500 feet, it became obvious that we were drifting sharply to the east. Static electricity was building up on the aircraft, affecting our ability to receive homing facilities. Also by this time, in-flight turbulence was becoming pretty severe.

"We reached the Shingbwiyang homer okay but only after drifting well to the east of the facility. Prior to takeoff the weather service had given us winds aloft of SW at approximately 75 miles per hour. I had corrected for that wind in flying to Shingbwiyang. It obviously was not enough. I computed the winds aloft on my hand-held computer as best I could and figured them to be SW at 125 mph at my altitude. Shortly after leaving my first checkpoint, I picked up a wind drift correction for the new wind I had computed.

"It turned out my new wind drift correction was not enough. Our second checkpoint was Paoshan, about 130 miles to the southeast. We never found it. Shortly after leaving Shingbwiyang, the static electricity which had built up on our aircraft smothered all homing facility reception. After that, we were on our own—just floating through the skies, not knowing exactly where we were. We spent most of this time just trying to keep the aircraft right side up and trying to get a signal on some homing facility.

"After flying over an hour without any navigational aid, I finally decided to try a homing facility to the north of our intended course to get a cross-check. By good fortune it turned out we were directly over that facility. Because we were directly over the facility, we were able to receive it in spite of the static electricity. We had been blown about 65 miles north of course even after all the wind correction I had made. This facility was in western China and past the main Hump.

"With another compute of the wind on my computer, I again figured our wind and afterwards was able to get into Kunming without further trouble. I did not return home to Sookerating that night, the only flight I ever made after which I did not proceed directly back home after dropping off my cargo. And, no one else went back home either, to my knowledge. It is likely the actual winds aloft were southwest at around 200mph. None of this wind was reflected in surface weather reports.

"All our aircraft carried a long-range radio that was called a "liaison set," used by our radio operators to call in en route position reports and emergency situations. It could not be used for navigation. However, by holding the transmitting button down, it could be used to allow "direction finding" stations in Assam, India, and Yunnan, China, to triangulate on the signal and determine the approximate location of lost aircraft. We referred to this as 'calling for a steer.'

"During the time that we were looking for Paoshan, we listened to all frequencies used by the liaison sets, and they were all filled with emergency calls from aircraft over the Hump looking for help in locating their positions. The strong winds, together with aircraft being unable to receive their navigational facilities due to static electricity, resulted in aircraft being blown all over the Hump. Records show we lost nine aircraft in that night's operation.

"I mention all the detail of my flying this night because, with your uncle's flight about an hour behind me, my flight was his flight. This is what he went through. Completing the flight that night did not result as much from pilots' skills as just plain luck. Your uncle's flight was in the air behind me as we were trying to find Paoshan. I have no way of knowing if they ever called for a steer. Also, I have no idea if any records of aircraft that called for steers that night were made a matter of record. If records do exist, they would most likely be in the archives of the Army Airways Communication Service (AACS), if such an archive exists.

"There is one other thing. I have enclosed a portion of an aeronautical chart that shows the Kunming, China, area. Northeast of the Kunming area you will see Chanyi, which was the destination of your uncle's flight that night. Northwest of Chanyi, near the top center of the chart, you will see Lien San Po. Adjacent to that you will see an "X" that marks the spot the military has indicated your uncle's crew may have been located. The normal route of flight would have been over Kunming then direct to Chanyi. The location indicated is in keeping with the possibility the aircraft was blown north and east of its intended route, which was common with all aircraft lost that night.

"I wish I could be of more help to you in your search. I further wish you the very best in your efforts to use DNA to identify your uncle. Please let me know if I can be of any further assistance to you."

Sincerely,

J. V. Vinyard

▶The "computer" Vinyard referred to was probably a "Type D Time-Distance Computer," the Army Air Corps' designation for a simple mechanical device. WWII, of course, predated the computer age.

Another fantastic person we met is Mr. Bryce Brand of Peoria, Illinois. He contacted me after reading a newspaper story by the Associated Press. Bryce had gone through two flying schools in Aviation Cadets with my brother and actually sent us the last known picture of him. To this day Bryce and I keep in contact. He has really helped me by answering questions about Harvey and his last days of life.

My daughter has also been able to locate Jackie Wellings, sister of 2nd Lt. Ray C. Taylor, who was the pilot my brother flew with on their final flight. We intend to keep in touch. We are still looking for a family member of the third crew member, Pvt. Robert R. Crowder, radio operator on the ill-fated flight.

My daughter feels she has traced my brother's remains to the Manila American Cemetery in the Philippines. With the help of Senator Feinstein, she has petitioned to have the remains exhumed and DNA tested. After one failed attempt, my daughter, again with the help of Senator Feinstein, appealed our case to the honorable Donald Rumsfeld, Secretary of Defense. He reviewed the case and has requested that the investigation be reopened.

Recently my husband and I attended the convention of the Hump Pilots Association in Washington, DC. It was a wonderful experience. No matter what the outcome of my search will be, I now feel at peace. My search has answered most of my questions and has connected me with many new friends.

So many brave young men lost their lives in that forgotten theatre, the CBI. Your book is one of the ways we can remember our loved ones. Because of these men and all men and women who served in World War II, we can now live in the greatest country in the world. Let us never forget. God Bless America.

Sincerely,
Gladie De Fouw,
Proud sister of 2nd Lt. Harvey Bos

"I got through
flying school
because I
figured I had
a job to do."
2nd Lt. Harvey Bos

Salina, KS

Dear Carl,

I really enjoyed your book. Fran has finally convinced me to put down a bit about my adventures in India. I have very little writing experience, but I am lucky to have kept my diary. By thumbing through it, I could uncover a few adventures, and that's what I've included here.

The last part of this letter is a tribute to a brother-in-law who was in on the Normandy landings.

Before getting into the CBI story, may I tell you about my early flying. I was drafted in the second Selective Service drawing, and I was sworn in at Leavenworth, Kansas, on July 15, 1941. My first assignment sent me to the 82nd Observation Squadron, US Army Air Corps, Salinas, California. I received an appointment to flying cadets soon after Pearl Harbor and in March 1942 entered pre-flight school at Santa Ana, California. After flight training at Vasalia-Danube, Chico, and Victorville, all in California, I received my wings and commission with the class of 42-I on September 22.

After two month flying Ferry Command out of Long Beach, I was transferred to Kansas City to train for six weeks with TWA. In January 1943 I was transferred to Braniff Airways in Brownsville, Texas. Learning mainly navigation and emergency procedures, we flew copilot for Braniff pilots, hauling passengers and cargo to the Panama Canal on C-47s. Three months later it was on to Homestead Field, Florida, for transition training on the C-46.

Next came a crew assignment and a trip to Fairfield, Connecticut, to pick up a new C-46 and fly it to Miami. My crew consisted of James Spurlock, copilot, and Jim Scroggie, navigator, along with a radio operator and flight engineer. On July 14, 1943, we left Miami, bound for India. Four of the five planes in the group were flown by Air Corps crews; the fifth was piloted by an airline pilot with an Air Corps crew. To give each crew the experience of long-distance navigation and other procedures, the planes took off in ten-minute intervals.

Our route was Puerto Rico; Georgetown; Belem, Brazil; Natal, Brazil (blowing sand, terrible food, but nice quarters and a dance band); Ascension Island (bare lava rock, absolutely no vegetation); Accra, Gold Coast, Africa (saw a funeral, loin cloths, naked kids, street dancers, the whole bit, missed by one day seeing on old friend from Cadets, Tom Nowling); Kano, Africa; Khartoum, Africa; Aden, Arabia (dusty, windy, smelly); Mesira Island; Karachi, India (billeted in a maharaja's palace, met friend Woods from Visalia); Agra, India (beautiful Taj Mahal, amazing Red Fort with 70 foot-thick inner walls, secret quarters for the Shah's three wives of different religions); Gaya, India; finally on August 1, Chabua, our base and destination. On the last leg of my long journey, Gaya to Chabua, there were two Chabua pilots with whom I became fast friends—Jug Wood and CD Williams. CD had been copilot on the C-46 from which correspondent Eric Severeid and twenty other men bailed out in the Ft. Hertz valley. They all survived and walked out, with the help of two medics who parachuted in to assist them.

Now, about my time in the CBI. To begin—amazingly, all five planes arrived in Chabua within a few hours of each—a record, I believe. My total flying time from Miami was 90:45. To greet us, we were told that a C-46 with twenty-three men on board went down about forty minutes east of Chabua. Chabua was hot as hell—malaria fever area, damp the year round, frogs and toads everywhere, 32-volt lighting, poor food (bread tasted like a damp dishrag), toilet facilities at a new low.

Four days later I was scheduled for my first Hump flight. It was not to be. The liaison transmitter went out, so the pilot returned to the field. Flight time? 1:40, Chabua to Chabua. Two days later I made it over the Hump. I was copilot to Flight Officer D. W. Muir. Until we got over Kunming, we were on instruments. After the plane was ready for the return to Chabua, Muir took the right seat and said, "Okay, Nethaway, you're a first pilot now." From that trip on, I was a first pilot for all my 70 round-trips until I departed Chabua on 2 July 1944. That was more than any other Hump pilot had achieved to that date. Radio operators and crew chiefs/flight engineers usually had more.

My next two flights were also on instruments. My first glimpse of the mighty Himalayas came on the return trip of my third flight. We had remained overnight in Yunnanyi because night flying of the Hump had not yet been authorized. I remember how beautiful the snow-capped mountains were.

My 22nd trip was eventful, to say the least. Early in the flight we had a complete failure of the radio compass (direction finder) and depended upon bearings and directions from Chabua. After four hours of flying (the flight to Kunming was normally three hours), I was ordered to continue east for another two and one-half hours! I protested vigorously—I knew I was already east of my destination, Kunming. Finally we prevailed. The airways realized their mistake and ordered us to fly west this time, another two and one-half hours. Of course we ran out of gas. We were 100 miles east of Kunming, I learned later.

We'd been on top at 11,000 feet with mountain peaks poking up through the clouds. We bailed out, descending through several thousand feet of clouds. We hit ground on a cultivated slope about 8,500 feet above sea level. We were extremely lucky. Within five hours the five of us were together. No one was injured. We were able to spend that first night in a tiny barn, sleeping on piles of rice. We were especially fortunate that a local school teacher, recently from Shanghai, and his servant volunteered to lead us to safety. He had a small book of English-Chinese translations, so we communicated by pointing to English words. Imagine our good luck—they stayed with us for five days, when we came to a small village. After that, ragtag provincial soldiers took turns leading us. At one point we climbed a 9,000-foot-steep pathway and descended to the other side. In the final village the town banker put us up for two days. He called our base at Chanyi on the phone, and soon a 6 by 6 truck with several soldiers came and took us to Chanyi. We hopped a ride to Kunming the next day, and the following day deadheaded back to Chabua. We missed the big Thanksgiving dinner, but so what!

I didn't keep a diary of our walkout, but I remember well some of the huts we stayed in on our journey. Joined to the huts were shelters and stalls for small horses, pigs, and other animals. The smell was overpowering. Animal and human waste was poured into a trench along the foundation of the huts. Rain kept it a fluid mess. The Chinese natives dipped it out with buckets tied to poles and poured it (lovingly) at the base of their meager crops. Bandits pillaged the villages constantly, and we would have been a juicy plum to be turned over to the Japs in the south. Again, we were lucky.

At every stop along the walkout, the soldiers picked out two to carry our heavy winter clothes, our boots and parachutes. They all carried on in protest. I remember one especially. At the noon stop, he came to me and showed me his foot, which had been cut clean across just back of the ball of the foot. Someone had sewn it closed with blue denim thread from old clothes; the stitches were broken and pulled apart. I talked to our guide and told him to release this guy to go home. Surprisingly, he did. I will never forget this one Chinaman's anguish, then his expression of gratitude to me, his face lighting up like a child's on Christmas.

Unlike Hump flights a year later, our flights from Chabua flew on a bearing of 97 degrees to Ft. Hertz and from there 117 degrees to Kunming. This northerly route was necessary because the Japanese were a threat, pretty well north in Burma. It meant flying over higher Himalayan peaks than a more southerly route, more violent winds and down drafts due to deep river gorges enclosed by high steep ridges. En route from Ft. Hertz I used to try to hit the center or the north tip of Lake Tali. Leaving Kunming field, just to the west of the lake and the strip, was a pagoda cut into the face of the thousand-foot cliff. In 1982 Fran and I traveled to China. In Kunming for a couple days, we walked a steep mountain path to visit this shrine. What a view! What a reminiscence for me!

At the end of my year on the Hump I was transferred to Karachi to fly the new Rocket Run supplying the new B-29 bases north of Calcutta with spare parts and engines.

One variation to Hump flying came on February 28, 1944. Together with nine other crews and planes, I was assigned to a British outfit in Chittagong to fly oats for pack mules, amo, and food to drop zones in the Akyab. A British unit pressing south in Burma had become surrounded by Japanese troops. These were short trips, low-altitude para-drops. The oats were double-bagged and dropped free on low passes. All the other supplies were parachuted, with British soldiers as kickers. It usually required four passes over the zone to kick out our 12,000 pounds. I recall one zone was a flat area, about a half-mile long on top of a ridge. At the end of the run was a lone tall tree with sparse leaves. There was a Jap sniper near the top of the tree, and on every pass I'd fly lower than the tree and lift the one wing just enough to clear it. By the third pass, he was gone. Those two R2800 engines are thunderous at full throttle. On March 5 we returned home to Chabua.

I've dwelt at some length in this letter about my small part in WWII. Let me now acknowledge that if I had to do it all over, I would change nothing. Would I exchange my assignment for a trek across North Africa and on up through Italy? I don't think so.

Let's consider life and danger on an aircraft carrier—an armorer, an airplane mechanic, a cook, or any of several thousand sailors deep in the bowels of the ship. The ship comes under air attack or is engaged by subs or battleships. The decks above are afire, explosions set off minute by minute. Imagine those hours of terror as the crew goes about its assigned tasks.

Or suppose you are in a submarine. Several destroyers are circling above you, dumping depth charges.

Or suppose you are in a landing craft, churning toward some heavily fortified South Pacific beach or making a rough ocean crossing on to Normandy Beach. Already seasick, you are ordered to storm the beach. If you make it that far, you reel in fear as you anticipate weeks and months of hand- to- hand fighting, ferreting the enemy out of their lava rock tunnels in the Pacific, fighting hedge row to hedge row, house to house in France and Germany.

Or you are in a bomber crew over Germany. A fighter has knocked your plane out and you are forced to bail out over enemy territory. Picture the terror of being a prisoner of war or, even worse, being forced to march on a death march.

I stand in absolute awe of these men. We had barracks and beds to sleep in every night, hot meals, showers, clean sheets, movies, candy, beer, and sunshine. They had snow or intense heat, mud, dirty clothes, C-rations, and lonely weeks and months in foxholes under heavy, relentless shelling or motor fire.

I thank God for my job on the Himalayan Hump.

Carl, I regret that it isn't in me to write a book. But at least I have this brief WWII memoir and some memorabilia to leave to my nephews and absolutely terrific grand nephews and nieces.

Thanks again for writing Born to Fly the Hump.

Sincerely,
Richard Nethaway

"A C-46 failed to make it off the North strip, Myitkyina, with a load of high octane." October 1945. (Bottoms)

Port Charlotte, FL

Dr, Constein,

I was a pilot stationed at Misamari from January 1944 to November 1944. As you well know, we didn't have fixed crews, so I have no record of the crew on my flight of October 14-15, 1944. I wish I could contact them. The flight—Misamari, India, to Chengkung, China, and return—was my 50th; just short of 600 hours logged, it was to be my last before heading stateside. It almost was my last—totally!

It happened on takeoff on the return trip to India. It was early Sunday morning, still dark. As the gear retracted, the left side of the C-46 lit up like a blowtorch. The wing was on fire! I instinctively pulled the extinguisher, throttled back, turned to the right toward the lake, and, only 500 feet off the ground, nursed the plane around for an approach. Over the end of the runway I called "Gear Down." Of course that wasn't possible because the hydraulic fluid had dumped into the exhaust stream, causing the fire in the first place. The crew chief anticipated the problem. He stood by with one of the extra cans of fluid we carried to make up for the leaks in the C-46's plumber's nightmare and poured all the fluid into the tank as I continued on the final approach. It worked. The gear came down. I shut down both engines as we rolled to a stop. We exited via the rear steps, and fire trucks extinguished the remaining fire. We took a look. The under side of the left wing was burned away. We could see the spars. The plane was a total loss. Why it didn't blow up or come apart in the air I will never know.

We deadheaded back to Misamari on the next plane. Base Operations had listed us as crashed and written us off as dead, as several Hump pilots in the air around Kunming at that time had seen the fire light up the sky. My basha mates (Pipkin and Hancock) were sorting out my stuff.

Six days later I left the theater to return to the US, lucky to be alive.

Robert Friedman

▶Bob had earlier told this story in the Hump Pilots Association Newsletter.

Vero Beach, FL

Dear Carl,

As you may remember from our conversation last winter when you and Millie visited me, I was based at Chanyi on the China side. Early in February, 1945, we were assigned to pick up a load of supplies at Myitkyina, Burma. Someone goofed: they didn't have anything for us and sent us on to your base of Chabua, India. There a driver backed his truck into our C-47 on the flight line and damaged an aileron. It took the rest of the day to repair the plane.

Our return flight from Myitkyina was destined for Chengkung, China. The flight would normally have been to our home base of Chanyi, but it was socked in. The next day we left Chengkung—not for Chanyi, which was still closed, but again for Myitkyina. (Beginning to sound like a comedy, isn't it?) We RONed in Myitkyina and left the next day—again for Chengkung because Chanyi was STILL closed. The date was Friday, February 9. Chengkung again sent us back to Myitkyina, and it was on this leg that we ran into trouble and had to bail out.

We had estimated our ETA at five hours. The weather was terrible—severe turbulence, ice snow, lightning. (I wasn't in the air during the famous Hump storm of January 6-7 just a month earlier, but the conditions sound similar.) Many planes called Maydays. We were flying at the unusually high altitude of 25,000 feet and pushed even harder to get on top at 27,500 feet. When we were an hour beyond our ETA, we too called a Mayday and requested a radio bearing. No luck. Low on fuel, six hours out, we knew we had no choice—we had to jump. It was 10:30 p.m.

I put on my jungle vest, jacket, pistol, and took cigarettes, matches, candy bars, and a whistle. We set the auto pilot at 16,700 feet and shook hands. Robey ordered Smarco to go first. Smarco went to the door, shook his head then backed away. Robey again ordered him to jump. This time he did, head first. Robey motioned to me. I gulped and stepped out. I caught a glimpse of red and green wingtip lights as I tumbled end over end. I started to count to ten but got only to three! I yanked the ripcord and all hell broke loose. Pain mixed with relief when the chute opened. A beautiful sight. I breathed a heavy sigh of relief.

I fell through the clouds. Everything was quiet and peaceful, but very black. I whistled and thought I got a whistle in reply. I saw the contour of a hill, covered my face with my hands and suddenly—WHAM!

I was on my stomach in a group of small trees, the chute folding on itself on the other side of the trees. I heard running water. We learned later we had landed on the east side of the Salween River, probably 10 miles north of the Burma Road Bridge.

I got up, removed the chute harness, and walked to the chute. The shrouds were hopelessly tangled in the trees, so I cut them off, rolled up in the chute in the hope of sleeping until morning. I was nearly asleep when the wind picked up and it began to rain. The rain subsided and I fell asleep. Again the wind blew hard. It was the longest night of my life, alternating between fitful sleep and scary wakefulness in a bed of mud.

Early the next morning, as I laid the chute out to dry, two young Chinese boys and three girls approached, jabbering away furiously. I broke off pieces of a peanut bar for them. They smiled and giggled. Using sign language I got across to them that I was hungry and wished to go to their home. Their hut was made of straw and bamboo and had a dirt floor. The old man of the house was making a kettle of rice and peas. It tasted all right, but the children had a hilarious time watching me struggle with chop sticks. Later came a piece of cheese, the hottest thing I have ever had in my mouth, followed by eggs. I showed them Glenna's and Susan's pictures. They all enjoyed that.

I tried to express my thanks, then returned to the chute, retrieved my whistle and blew it. Not far away, Smarco answered. Soon he and Robey found me.

Smarco and Robey went to the house where I had been and after a short time returned with a Chinese captain who said he would take us to a village with an ATC base nearby. In mid-afternoon the Chinese loaded wood on four cows, our chutes on another and off we went, heading east. The walk was extremely strenuous—up sharp passes then down again. The high altitude, probably a mile high, took its toll on our endurance.

The whole town turned out to greet us, grinning and chanting, "Ding How!" "Ding How!" We were taken to one house which had a fireplace in the center of the room for cooking. The meal was rice. Then we were led to a house which had two stories. There must have been about 10 Chinese fussing over us and tucking us in for the night. In spite of the hard beds, we slept like babies.

The following day a new crew of Chinese people took over and conducted us over even higher mountains, perhaps 9,000 feet high, still heading east. On this second day, after passing many rice paddies, we finally arrived at another village and were taken to a Chinese major. He took us to his room and fed us with the usual fare, augmented by a big bowl of greens, probably spinach, with squares of either meat fat or dough. It was tough to get down. Then it was bedtime. What a good sign it was to see US Army blankets on our beds!

The next morning the Major and a Chinese Colonel greeted us. We communicated by means of an English-Chinese phrase book I had in my jungle pack. The two accompanied us, most of us on horseback, the boys carrying our chutes. After an hour we came out on the Burma Road. Again a welcome sign of relief—US Army tire tracks on the dirt road! The two Chinese officers shook our hands and left. They did not accept the money we offered them.

An hour later a jeep and trailer came down the road. We hitched-hiked a ride and about 4:00 p.m. arrived at the 21st US Army Field Hospital, Paoshan. Incidentally, a doctor there was a fine young fellow from your fair city of Reading, Pennsylvania. We spent a week there because the grass airfield was too soft for a C-47 to take off. The stay was pleasant—soft beds, hot water, good food, movies every other night, and plenty of needed rest.

After seven days we were flown back to our home base at Chanyi. You know, it's strange, but I can recall details of this 55-year-old adventure better than I remember most current stuff.

Let me end with a disturbing sequel to my bailout. Glenna was immediately notified that I was missing and would be paid from the Missing Persons Division. She was of course very upset. Fortunately, she was able to get good stateside help, and after four days she was notified that I had been found safe and sound.

Best regards to
a good Hump friend,
Bill Boreman

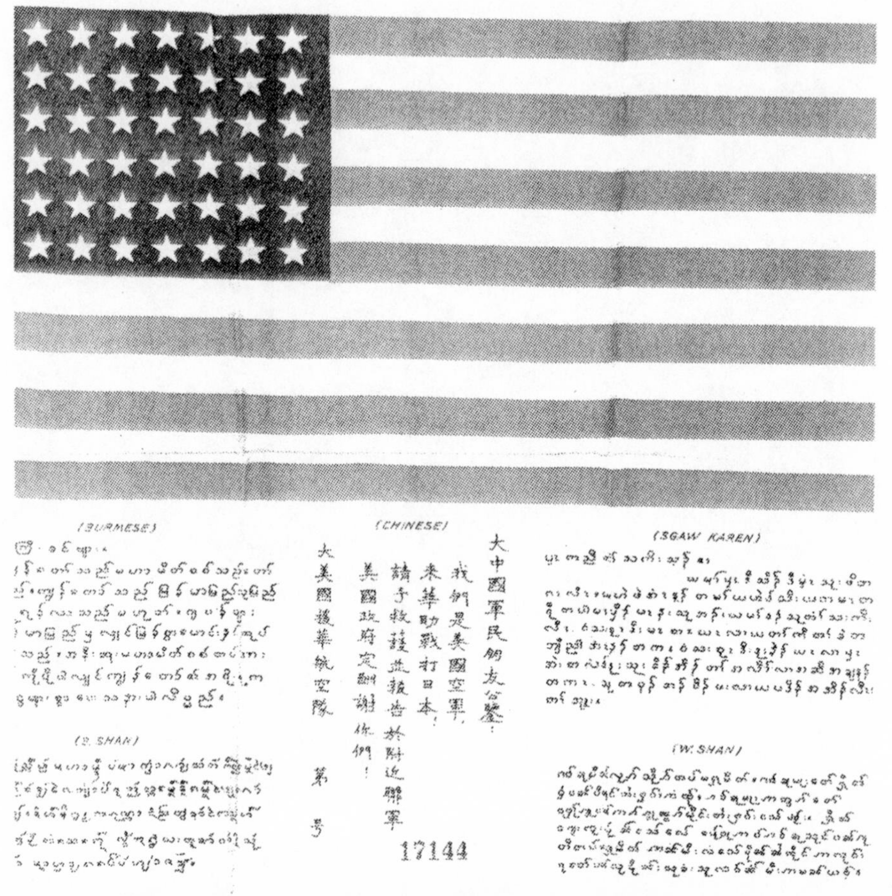

Leather chits inside their flight jackets identified downed airmen as Americans. The message requested food and asked to be taken to the nearest Allied military post, adding there would be a reward, (From Bill Boreman)

Rutland, MA

Dear Carl,

Charles Shultz's Snoopy used to begin his adventures with, "It was a dark and stormy night." Snoopy may have been describing my Hump flight of June 28, 1945, even though it began in the daytime, at

1400 hours. The date and times are in my logbook; the flight itself is clear in my memory.

Loaded with gasoline, our C-109 left Shamshernagar, India, for Chengtu, China. Our assigned altitude was 19,000 feet. Gasoline was the only cargo I ever took to China over the Hump in C-109s or C-54s. On most C-54 return trips we ferried soldiers on rotation to Dum Dum (Calcutta).

June was the middle of the monsoon season; the weather was rainy but the flight in the stratus clouds was fairly smooth in the beginning. But as we neared the First Ridge, it got very dark, with frequent lightning to brighten things up.

For the next five hours we were tossed about, thrown and beaten by hail, rain, and severe turbulence. St Elmo put on his fiery show. We fought our way through at least five monster storms. My copilot and I flew the plane manually, for I never used automatic pilot in IFR condition. We landed in Chengtu seven and a half hours after takeoff in India.

While the plane was being unloaded, we went to the mess hall for either stuffed peppers or China's famous "egg-us" —my memory fails me which. For the return trip Operations assigned us an altitude of 21,000 feet and warned us about severe cumulonimbus storms over the main Hump. Of course we knew that, but we took off anyway. About half-way back, about at Yunnanyi, the ride became so rough my copilot got airsick. I couldn't help him because I was frantically trying to keep the plane on an even keel.

After we crossed the Ridge, things improved and the sky got brighter. The turbulence decreased and the copilot felt better. We broke out on top, and the rest of the trip was uneventful. Flying time on the return flight was five hours, five minutes. We landed back at Shamshernagar at 0420 hours after the wildest ride in my life.

Sincerely,
Loring G. Briggs (Larry)

Short Takes on the Monster Storm of January 6 - 7, 1945

■ Bill Watts (Tuscon, AZ): *I flew out of Misamari and made the famous January 6 day. Our field lost three planes.*

■Bill Sackett (Haskell, NJ): *Flying a C-46 with Troop Carrier, I too was up in that January storm. Looking forward to reading your account.*

■ Col. Jack Tamm - Retired (Daytona Beach, FL): *Like you, I made 96 round-trips on the Hump, including the January 6, 1945, trip. My return cargo that day consisted of young Chinese men destined to be trained as pilots in the USA. What an indoctrination flight for them.*

■ John Meek (Ketchum, OK): *A civilian pilot, I was recruited by the Army, eventually flying the C-54 out of Tezgaon. I too flew in that storm.*

■ Don Bean (Portland, OR): *I flew out of Sookerating and remember well the January storm.*

■ John Wilson, Capt., EAL, Ret. (Sanbornton, NH): *I remember well the wx of the January 6 storm. We beat it back to Jorhat on the fifth and reported it.*

■ Jay Warner (Rochester, NY): *I recall the storm of January 6. A few Chabua guys came back after throwing out their cargos. Said they were blown on top. Incidentally, I topped you by three trips. I had 99 before going to Gaya to instruct.*

■ Nelson Beck (North Warren, PA): *A radio operator on C-46s, I ended up with 809 hours and over 100 missions. My log shows I was on a two-day mission a day or so before January 6. Lucky!* ▶ Beck informed me his father passed away in August, 2001.

■ Jim Calvert (San Antonio, TX): *I was Operations Officer at Kunming the night of the big storm. The crews that came in that night were physically and emotionally shook up.*

■ Howard Randol (Capistrano Beach, CA): *I arrived in Misamari the day after the big storm. We had lost eight planes.*

■ Tom Manning (Higden, AZ): *I flew C-46s out of Chabua, as you did. I was the last pilot to leave the base—December 4, 1945. On January 6 the wind was out of the South at 110 mph. I carried a 45-*

degree correction and was an hour and a half overdue reaching Kunming. I made 85 round-trips, none worse than that.

■ Lt. Col. Jack Pipkin (Vacaville, CA): *I landed at your field of Chabua a few times during my tour in India. My most memorable landing there was an emergency when I was low on gas after flying through the granddaddy of all storms.*

■ Col. Jean Nutty (Oklahoma City, OK): *I also flew the night of the Big Storm. One thing about flying the Hump—you came back a much better pilot. It's not too surprising we never met, for there wasn't much time for socializing.*

■ Bob Van Buskirk (Aurora, CO): *Our C-54 got kicked around the night of January 6. But that was tolerable—until #3 engine came unglued. We made it into the RAF base at Sylhet. (C-54 copilot called the Lord for help. The Lord came back: "Son, I'm so busy with those poor C-46 and CNAC boys. You four-engine guys are on your own.")*

■ Ed Randell (Cameron Park, CA): *On January 6 I flew a C-87 from Jorhat to China and back. On that return flight, we were blown north off course toward Tibet and were low on fuel. After getting a radio fix from Calcutta, we headed for Tezpur for fuel. After we broke out of the clouds, I saw a mountain dead ahead. I told the weather officer at Jorhat that we had 200 mph headwinds. His reply: "The wind never blows that hard!"*

La Quinta, CA

Dear Carl,

I just finished reading your interesting book on flying the Hump. It brought back my own experience flying out of Tezpur and Jorhat, an exciting year in my 45- year career as pilot.

I noted in your first chapter that for you, flying was a means of getting the best deal you could in the service. For me, flying has been my life from the time my father set me loose to solo at age 16. A WWI pilot, he had come home to California after the war to earn his living flying—barnstorming, air shows, charter flights, airline pilot, and owning a flying school. That solo was a thrill I shall never forget. Two years later I obtained a Commercial license and a Flight

Instructor's rating. I began instructing and getting paid for it! I would have done it for nothing, just for the sheer joy of flying.

A year after Pearl Harbor, 1000 hours under my belt, I applied to be a ferry pilot with the 6th ATC Ferry Command at Long beach. I was accepted into the Army Air Corps as 2nd Lt. and proudly donned the silver wings. I was put right into Transition and instructed in C-47s, C-46s, B-25s, B-17s, and B-24s. After nearly two years, my pleasant, rather carefree life as aviator came to an abrupt halt when I received orders for overseas duty—destination India, the "Hump."

Carl, I thoroughly appreciated your narrative on the historic Hump day of January 6-7, 1945. As I recall, you also flew into Luliang that day. If I may, I'd like to tell you my experience on that eventful day. Before that, a word about Service Pilots. I was sorry to read in your memoir that you had some bad experiences with some of these lads you were assigned to assist in route familiarization. Of course that coin has two sides. As a Service Pilot myself, I discovered when I got to Tezpur that the CO was taken into the service as a Captain because of his business background, age and flying experience. Yes, he was also a Service Pilot. He later changed his wings, as I did.

Now, the January 6-7 story. My trip was out of Tezpur in a C-87 to Luliang. We started getting into the weather over the First Ridge, the Naga Hills, with the usual St. Elmo's Fire and ice flying off the props and banging into the fuselage. As we approached Myitkyina at our cruising altitude of 18,000 feet, we were suddenly sucked down two or three thousand feet, unable to hold altitude even with the engines set for maximum power. Then just as suddenly we were propelled upward at 4,000 feet per minute right on through our assigned altitude to 22,000 feet. The turbulence was so violent we were having trouble keeping the airplane right side up. Everything in the cockpit that was not secured, including a fire extinguisher, was flying through the air.

After another half hour of this wild ride, we flew over Kunming twenty minutes ahead of our flight plan. We landed at Luliang and noticed more C-47s, C-46s, and C-87s parked on the ramp. Operations was crowded with crews who had just come through the same weather we had, and of course they did not want to return to India through the same weather. We listened as one of the pilots told the base commander on the phone that in 20 years of flying with the airlines, he had never flown through weather more violent. Nobody, he said, should be required to fly back until the weather cleared. The base commander told him he could not countermand orders from headquarters (The Mill, Calcutta): "The Hump will not be closed due to weather." So we all filed our flight plans and took off to the west for our bases in India.

Hoping to miss some of the weather, we chose to fly back on the more northerly "Able" course at an altitude of 23,000 feet. The higher altitude was a good idea, but the northerly course was not, for the wind now was out of the south at over 100 mph, blowing us even farther north. When we passed Mt. Tali, all hell broke loose—an elevator ride as before but much more turbulent. After about 15 minutes we were tossed like a toy out of the storm at 32,000 feet. There the air was silky smooth and the sky above was clear. Stars were shining brightly.

Because of radio static and interference, we were unable to ascertain our position, although we had a pretty good idea we were far north of our course. And how! Finally, after another hour when we picked up a weak signal from Ft. Hertz, we changed our heading from west to nearly south and followed an aural null to Ft. Hertz. We had been so far north over the peaks of the higher Himalayas, it scared me to contemplate what would have happened had we been flying at a lower altitude. Many planes are still sitting on snow-capped peaks north of the "Able" course.

As you know, Carl, the weather was the main enemy. But I had two experiences with Japanese "Betty" twin-engine bombers over the Hump as well. On a clear moonlight night, February 20, 1945, returning to India on the Able course, a single Betty pulled up closely on our tail and began firing on us. We were directly over the mighty Salween River gorge at the time, so I rolled the C-87 right over on its back and did a power-on "split-S" straight down, exceeding the airspeed redline and praying that the wings would stay on. We rolled out on a southerly heading following the Salween River, which was visible in the moonlight. The mountains on each side of the river were also visible, above us now as we leveled off at about 9,000 feet. The Betty did not follow us; I guess he figured we were goners.

On another occasion 10 days after the monster storm of January 6-7, 1945, we took off from Chengtu for Tezpur during a "three-ball" alert.

As we turned south for our on-course climb, there appeared a mass of red and green wing lights heading our way. There was no time for evasive action. We flew right through the middle of a formation of five Bettys, three on our right wing and two on our left, with less than 50 feet of clearance on either side. They were diving on the airport that we had just departed. We increased the power on those four Pratt & Whitney engines to war emergency and climbed into the overcast above to escape one of the Bettys which decided to come after us. The Bettys did indeed bomb the airport and destroyed a couple planes parked on the ramp.

A most interesting sequel to this story occurred in 1958, just 13 years later. I was flying as pilot for the newly-formed Japan Airlines on the domestic routes. We had an overnight layover in Chitose. Mr. Kaneda, copilot, and I had a drink together. During the conversation we discovered he was in Burma in WWII at the same time I was based in India. When he told me he had been flying Bettys then, I related my extraordinary experience with those bombers. He was amazed, for he not only had heard about the incident, he had also gotten first-hand information from his good friend and tent-mate—one of the Betty pilots in that formation!

From age 16 to age 60, flying was a most gratifying part of my life. I retired as an international airline pilot, flying B-747s. Flying the Hump will forever be one of the most memorable years of my career in the sky.

Warmest regards,
Joseph B. Plosser

Adah, PA

Dear Carl,

You and I have two things in common—both of us were Hump pilots in WWII and both superintendents of schools in Pennsylvania after the war. The CBI experience that separates us was my bailout.

I had been flying C-46s out of Mohanbari next door to you at Chabua, with trips to Kunming, Yunnanyi, and Chengtu. On October 23, 1943, one year before you arrived in Chabua, we were en route to Kunming with a cargo of 45-caliber ammunition. Our crew was 1st Lt. Tom Withers, pilot; Sgt. William Dhooghie, crew chief; Cpl. Wesley French, radio operator. I was copilot. Suddenly, out of nowhere came several Japanese Zeros; we were under attack. They attacked us from the rear and beneath our C-46. Even though it was a CAVU day, we never saw them from the cockpit.

Their first pass sounded like someone throwing handfuls of pebbles against the fuselage. We were losing oil pressure in the left engine. Tom ordered Dhooghie back to the cabin to get a better look. The engine began to smoke. As he came back to report, machine gunfire hit the cargo bay. Suddenly a burst came up through the cockpit floor. We saw daylight through the hole. I felt a sting in my left leg. French had blood oozing out his cheek. Dhooghie's face was crimson red from being peppered by metal fragments. In ten minutes it was all over. Tom gave the order to bail out. He said he would try to set the autopilot and then get out himself.

Dhooghie forced open the cargo door and, with flames shooting out the left engine, the three of us took turns jumping. As I jumped I saw the bottom of the tail section pass over my head. When we were attacked we were flying at 17,000 feet. We had dropped about 2,000 feet during the attack, and the tops of the mountains were about 10,000 to 12,000 feet.

When my chute opened, I felt so strong a jolt I thought my neck had snapped. But what a welcome feeling to be floating earthward! That feeling soon passed when I heard the roar of a plane in a dive, its props revving. He came streaking toward us as we were falling into a valley. I grabbed my left riser and spilled the air out of my chute in order to fall faster. I looked right down into his cockpit as he passed. He turned toward Dhooghie and French, who were on my left. We were very lucky—he missed us all.

We landed near in an area where the Japanese army had recently made a thrust into north Burma. I heard voices approaching. I feared a Japanese patrol. Fortunately, they turned out to be friendly Kachins. I showed them the American and Chinese flags sewn inside my flight jacket. They appeared to understand and nodded their heads. The chief took me to the village at the base of the ridge. Soon Dhooghie and French were brought in. We were happy to be together, but we were worried about Tom, for we had not spotted a fourth chute.

Later in the day we lay on the floor of a hut to which we were assigned. The natives were cooking around a campfire and offered us food. We thanked them but preferred the emergency food from our backpacks.

At around nine that night we were shocked to hear loud barking of dogs. We saw a light approaching our hut and again feared a Japanese patrol. We drew our 45s and waited. The door opened, light flooded into the room. There was a tense moment. Then we heard, "Don't shoot, it's me—Tom." What a happy moment for us all! Tom told us that before he bailed out he had returned to the cockpit for a flashlight. The delay carried him over the next ridge. He was not as lucky in his landing as the rest of us had been. He landed in a tall tree and broke an ankle when he climbed down.

As we discovered, those high mountain valleys are very cold at night. All we had to cover us was our chutes. We spent the next day trying to use sign language to communicate with the Kachin natives. They kept making signs and pointing to the sky, indicating how small we had been in the sky and how large we were on earth. For the second day we ate our emergency rations, but we realized that if we were going to get out, we would have to eat the food the natives offered us. We endured a second frigid night.

What a shock we were in for the next day. Into the village walked a stocky Kachin native carrying a Thompson Machine gun! His name was Diraminin. He understood and spoke some English and told us he had served as gun bearer for the British Army in Burma. He told us we would have to move out the next morning, as the Japanese Army was approaching. He arranged for natives to carry Tom on a bamboo stretcher. He led us to the next village. He asked us to write our names on a slip of paper and told us he would send a message. We wondered how he would do that. We learned later that he was assigned to a rescue unit whose mission it was to assist downed American and British pilots and crews. His means of sending messages was to send out runners ahead of us.

We spent the next 14 days climbing and descending, climbing and descending treacherous mountain trails toward northwest Burma. In the higher mountain passes we had to rest often because of the lack of oxygen.

On the fifteenth day came the break we were praying for. We came to a village where we met a British captain and a Burmese doctor. They knew we were coming because the runner had reached them. Captain Milton told us he had sent a wireless message to his British unit informing them we were safe and were walking out. The British conveyed the message to our American base. Captain Milton also told us an airdrop of food and clothing would reach us in two or three days. Imagine our joy!

The following day our friend Diraminin returned to his own area. We thanked him heartedly and bid him a warm goodbye.

On the trail three days later we were met by a small mule train with shoes, sweaters, underwear, blankets, socks, trousers, and three cases of dehydrated mountain rations, which required the addition of water. Dr. Dee and Captain Milton walked with us for four or five days, after which we were passed on to Lt. Reberro, a Burmese political officer.

He arranged for natives to escort us for the next few days.

With better food and fresh, clean clothes, we returned to our routine of negotiating mountain trails. Finally we reached our destination—Ft. Hertz, the Army Corp base along the northern route of the Hump. A C-47 was waiting to fly us back to Chabua.

It had been a long, arduous 28 days. We had passed through 24 native villages, crossed several streams, and walked over two swinging bridges. We were told we probably covered over 275 miles. But we survived—thanks to the efforts of the US Army Air Corps, the British and Burmese armies, who jointly devised the rescue procedure. We made it!

It is ironic that after being shot down, my parents informed by telegram that I was MIA, going through debriefing—after all this nothing about it appeared on my personnel records or separation papers. We were told in debriefing we would probably receive the Purple Heart or Air Medal. But everything was lost in the paper shuffle.

Tom Withers was sent home to the USA for medical treatment. Bill Dhooghi and Wes French were transferred to other bases in India. My twelfth Hump flight was my last. I was transferred to Lalmanir Hat, India, from where I flew C-47s up and down the Assam Valley in all of 1944. I returned to the States on New Year's Day, 1945.

In 1991 I finally received my Purple Heart and Service Medals. My bailout and wound had been recorded on my last medical examination prior to my release from Active Duty and my assignment to the USAF Res. in January 1947.

Sincerely,
George J. Plava
Col. USAF Res. (Ret.)

►One crew from Chabua that bailed out over the Hump returned to tell us an amazing story. After many weeks recuperating as guests of a Kachin village, the crew was finally ready to set out on its return journey. As a going-away gift, the chief gave the 1st pilot a brand-new Japanese 35mm camera!

Scotch Plains, NJ

Hi Carl,

I'm not much of a writer, but I'd like to tell you a bit about my flying. My career began when I was a student at Waynesburg (PA) College, continued when I flew in the Army Air Corps in WWII, and ended after 34 post-war years flying for United Airlines.

CPT (Civilian Pilot Training) came to Waynesburg when I was a sophomore. As a freshman I had had my first airplane ride and was sure that what I wanted to be in civilian life was a pilot, not a CPA. I completed primary flight training and earned a private license. Then I ran into a snag—I was too young to qualify for the next class. I handled that, shall we say, in the obvious way. I had moved to Clarksburg, West Virginia, where I was flying Waco biplanes in the Secondary CPT program. When a CAA inspector caught the discrepancy between the date on my birth certificate and on my license, I fessed up. He was sympathetic.

I continued on to advanced training, flying the Stinson Reliant and Waco and Cub Cruisers. By spring of 1942 I had my Commercial license with Flight Instructor rating. My partner and I heard about a new Army Air Corps Primary Flight School in Tennessee. We went there and were hired as instructors. We flew around for several hours getting acquainted with the Stearman PT-17.

A new class arrived and cadets were lined up tallest to shortest, as we instructors were. The five tallest cadets were assigned to the tallest instructor, etc. We were paid $250 a month to start. Then Fairchild P-19s were brought in and we were offered $400 a month if we worked upper class in the morning, lower class in the afternoon. Not bad, but it didn't take me long to realize I didn't care for instructing.

I looked into the ferry command. As soon as I could be released by the Southeast Training Command I went to Romulus, Michigan, and was hired as a civilian. That was spring, 1943. I was checked out in the AT-6 and anything else that was available.

My first scheduled ferry flight was as copilot of a B-24. I walked out to the flight line, looked the plane over and started back to operations. The captain stopped me and asked who I was. I told him I was to be his copilot but I didn't even know how to turn the radio on. He told me to get my ass out there immediately. The engineer, he said, would show me what to do. I learned very fast. In 24 days I was copilot delivering four B-24s and a C-46 to fields throughout the country. After my commission and AAC Pilot rating came through, I was soon flying P-40s, P-39s, P-47s, P-51s, and P-63s. Checkouts on the pursuit planes was not exactly thorough—a cockpit check, shoot a couple landings, and head out!

Romulus pilots ferried Bell and Curtiss planes manufactured in Buffalo and Niagara Falls to fields throughout the country. We also flew P-39s and P-63s to Great Falls, Montana. From there Great Falls pilots ferried them to Alaska and turned them over to the

Russians. Occasionally, when Great Falls pilots were delayed by weather on the Alcan route, I got to fly to Alaska. On some multi-engine ferry flights I got checked out by making a couple landings en route.

A big change came my way in the fall of 1944. I was sent to Reno for C-46 training for the Hump. I already had C-46 ferry time, but because of its mountainous setting, Reno was a good location for Hump training. Besides that, Reno was a great place to be based for a couple months. It was a small, Saturday-night type of town, the divorce capital of the country. When we were in town, we'd head for the train station to check out the lovely divorce-seekers who arrived on the afternoon train every day.

After my training in Reno I was on orders to deliver a new C-46 to Karachi, India. The route from West Palm Beach was via South America, Africa, Misira Island. At one layover I ran into an old buddy who was on his way to the States after completing his tour on the Hump—IN FIVE MONTHS! He advised me to look up a Captain Kelso in Karachi and ask for an assignment to the base at Misamari because I could get a lot of flying time there and complete my Hump tour quickly, as he had done.

My buddy was right. Misamari was an efficient operation, run like an airline. In fact, the CO was a United Airlines pilot in civilian life, Col. Claron Pratt.

Our main cargo was 55-gallon drums of gasoline. At high altitude the drums sometimes leaked like a fountain. When that happened, we threw them overboard. Every time I watched one of Uncle Sam's $2000 investments fall, I thought, "There goes my new Buick convertible."

Things were going well. I was close to the required 350 hours for rotation home. Then the shoe dropped—the requirement was raised to 500. I was almost there when it was raised again to 750 hours, and later to 1,000 hours plus remaining in the CBI for one year! When the Hump operation itself and Misamari were closed, I was assigned to various bases in the valley, the last one being Dum Dum Airfield in Calcutta.

One memorable assignment I had there was flying bodies from the Hump base cemetery to a central burial ground in Calcutta. I soon found out why they emphasized bringing your oxygen mask for these *flights, even though we did not fly at high altitude. Another learning experience was ferrying a C-46 to Shanghai. En route I laid over in Kunming. I figured my $80 American would show me a good time. I exchanged it for Chinese money at the West China rate of 2000 to 1. When I arrived in Shanghai, the rate of exchange was 400 to 1. A US Navy fleet also arrived after being at sea for six months and suddenly the rate plummeted. I got out of there in a hurry and returned to India.*

Every Hump pilot had close calls. I had one which stands out in my mind. Returning to Misamari, India, from Kunming, China, empty, I was being given some sort of check ride by a captain in the right seat. He told me he needed only this round-trip to qualify to go home. At 20,000 feet we broke out of the clouds and stared ahead at one of those monster thunderstorms which dotted the Hump routes in the fall and winter. This one looked as though it was boiling, full of fire, and God knows how high. "We better try to go around this sucker," I said.

"No," he said, "hold your course. We'll go right through it." As check pilot of course he had command.

"Okay," I said, "I'll fly this thing. You keep the carburetors heated up and the engines running."

We were soon in the middle of the roughest turbulence I had ever flown in. After what seemed like hours, we were spit out of the storm at 18,000 feet, the right engine wind-milling. Soon we were back in the storm. Unable to start the engine, we feathered it. We lost altitude fast, finally able to stop our descent at 12,000 feet, which was 2,000 feet below the minimum altitude for this area. The night was totally black. A trailing wire antenna had become entangled with the antenna of our Automatic Direction Finder radio. I had no idea where we were. The radio operator saw us pull up our parachute harnesses and excitedly asked if we were going to bail. I said I didn't plan to but he could if he wanted to. He decided to stay.

So here we are—on instruments, flying in severe turbulence, not sure where we are, one engine shut down, and scariest of all, 2,000 feet below the peaks in the area. Then an idea flashed into my mind. I recalled a pilot friend telling me about a good radioman at Myitkyina, Burma, who on his own monitored ATC frequencies in bad weather on the Hump. His call sign was "Stoker." I called him on emergency frequency. He came right back with, "Give me a ten-second hum on your mic." I did and he came in with a heading to his base. We kept this up every 30 seconds until he gave us a screwy bearing, then a reciprocal. We knew we had passed over his station. We did a 180. We were still IFR. On the ground at Myitkyina, operations ordered a powerful magnesium flare lighted. We saw the glow, descended, broke out at 500 feet and landed safely. I was never known to be a religious man, but I did say a few prayers of thanks that night.

In February 1982 I retired from United. My Hump experience and my flying of many types of AAC planes was good experience. United's DC-8 was a snap.

Sincerely,
A. H. Miller

Novelty, OH

Carl,

Enjoyed reading your book Born to Fly the Hump.*Your description of the weather you and I encountered while traversing those mountains was certainly accurate and brought back some unforgettable memories.*

One night after leaving Chengtu we saw a solid bank of thunderstorms across the entire horizon, reaching, I would estimate, up to 60,000 feet. Young and naïve, we took a vote and elected to go through the storms rather than return to the base in China.

With the rate of climb indicator going from 500 feet up to 500 feet down and the altimeter almost spinning, my copilot and I were literally standing on the pedals trying to keep control. To this day, I think we virtually turned over in the air. A B-24 was not designed to fly upside down. After about 20 minutes we broke out on the other side of the storms. I asked our navigator where we were. He told me to make a 30-degree correction to the south. He was right.

On another night flight, this one from Ipin, China, we were cruising along peacefully. It was 4:00 a.m. All of us were tired and weary.

I was staring at the instruments, mesmerized. Suddenly I caught myself with my head nearly on my left knee. Instinctively I flipped the oxygen lever to full oxygen. That brought me back to full consciousness. I looked over to find the copilot sound asleep. Whether or not the rest of the crew was asleep I'm not sure, but I believe they were. You and I know what a slow spiral will do in the short run, and we were in a spiral to the left. On future flights the crew made sure they were completely alert.

In November I'll be talking to fourth graders about the CBI. Like you, I've addressed only adults and high school juniors and seniors until now. It will be an experience.

Carl, I was glad to hear that you knew my father, Albright College's Prof Gates. He was quite a guy.

Best regards,
Stan Gates

Cookeville, TN

Dear Carl,

I am eager to receive your book and renew those exciting times over the Hump. At age 78 I too am trying to get some things together into a book. Finishing it is not easy. I must get busy!

I was a B-17 radio operator-gunner in the Army Air Corps in Europe with 32 B-17 missions over Germany. Actually, for raids over Ploesti, Munich, Regensburg, and Vienna we were awarded double credit. Of course the flights were fraught with danger. But there was also some humor, as when a cook stowed away and flew a mission with us. He became so excited he accidentally pulled his ripcord. I can still picture him dragging his chute behind on the ground as he left the plane back in Italy. On another mission, the top turret gunner called out,"German fighters coming in high at 2 o'clock." We all strained to spot them. They turned out to be dirt specks on the plexiglass turret!

While I was in Europe my parents sent me a pocket-size Bible with a steel-plated cover. It was to be worn next to your heart. But it wasn't merely for physical protection, for my parents were pointing me to God's word for protection as well.

My second tour of duty sent me to far-away Assam, India, to fly the Hump on C-87s—actually B-24s converted to fly cargo. The danger there was not the enemy in the sky but flying over dense jungle and high Himalayan peaks in the world's worst weather. Between flying the Hump and combat, I would choose combat.

On June 6, 1945, we took off on a night flight to China from our base in Jorhat, India. Bill Montgomery was pilot. In about 20 minutes we were unable to climb. The engineer, J.W. Tharp, came to my position and pointed his flashlight at the leading edge of the wings. We were picking up thick, clear ice much faster than normal. Bill was unable to pull the plane above the icing. Number 4 engine went out, and the plane began to tilt from side to side. We stalled out and fell into a flat spin. Bill ordered us to quickly put on our chutes.

Al Arline, the copilot, jumped first. Bill stayed at the controls, buying precious time. The plane was plunging in a turn, pinning me to the floor. Finally I was able to get on my chute and fasten the straps. I reached the upper hatch and stuck my head out. I pulled up again and again but could not get out. I panicked. I thought I would surely die. Suddenly, I felt a hand under each foot, giving me a strong boost. Tharp had pushed me out! As I fell free, I followed the plunging plane with my eyes. It crashed in a terrible explosion.

As luck had it, Al and I were on the ground in friendly Kachin territory. Jang, the headman, spoke broken English. A day later another Hump pilot spotted our smoke signal and our mirror. He circled and took a bearing. The next day two B-25s from the search and rescue mission in Assam dropped supplies and a walkie-talkie. After 20 days in the jungle, much of it in a village called Htawgaw, we were rescued, flown out in a B-25.

I corresponded often with Jang. I was attempting to arrange for my kind and gracious host to visit me in the U.S. Then, sadly, news came of his death. My fellow survivor of that tragic crash, Al Arline, went home to Louisiana and started a crop-dusting service. He was killed in 1951 when his plane crashed and burned near Shreveport.

In 1949 the remains of Montgomery and Tharp were transferred from the CBI to the Fort Smith National Cemetery in Arkansas. I traveled there and located the common grave (two buried in one grave with one headstone or marker). I longed to see a fuller inscription than their name, rank, and date of death. I recalled an inscription honoring the men of Kohima, India, who died standing fast against a Japanese onslaught for 16 days:

When you go home,
Tell them of us and say,
"For their tomorrow
We lost our today."

Respectfully yours,
Jasper N. Bailey

▶ I was pleased to learn that it was Assam's Search and Rescue unit which was instrumental in the rescue of Bailey and Arline. As I said in my memoir *Born to Fly the Hump,* in my year at Chabua I was completely ignorant of the existence of this or any other organized Search and Rescue organization. But then, communication was not, apparently, high on the priority list, at least not at Chabua.

Avon, IN

Dear Carl,

Talking with you on the phone recently about your book Born to Fly the Hump *inspired me to write some of my experiences on the Hump. Like you, I was an ATC pilot flying the C-46 Curtiss Commando. I flew 89 round-trip flights out of Misamari, which is in the Upper Assam Valley, not far from the foothills of the mighty Himalayas. Also like you, I was stationed in India from November 1944 to December 1945. How suddenly and dramatically life had changed for me—just four months earlier I had married Melba Wippel, my childhood sweetheart. My most earnest wish was to get my time in and return home to her.*

My most hair-raising Hump trip was a night flight to China. The crew of three had not flown together before. Our cargo was twenty-two 55-gallon drums of gasoline for our fighters and bombers in China. After a normal takeoff and climb to cruising altitude, the weather began turning bad and IFR became the order of the day. We entered ominous cumulonimbus clouds and were immediately tossed about violently. The radio operator was busy sending and receiving messages, and the copilot held the carburetor heat levers steady as best he could. A bolt of lightening struck between the copilot and me. The props began running away. I put each prop in emergency fixed hold. They both held, thank God! I slowly decreased and increased the position to synchronize the engines. By this time, thick ice had formed on the wings and props. The leading edges of the wings looked like strips of brightly lighted neon and the props resembled circles of neon lights. We knew this was St. Elmo's Fire. From a control in the cockpit we shot alcohol to the props to break off the ice.

I was about to give the order to bail out when I saw on a cockpit indicator that the antenna used for long-range communication was deployed. Feeling that the good Lord was watching over us, knowing we were flying out of the worst of the storm, seeing no fire, I reduced the pitch of the props and aircraft speed in preparation for landing at Kunming.

We landed without incident. We ate our Chinese "egg-is," the plane was unloaded, the props and radio equipment were repaired, and we took off for our home base of Misamari. We were all happy to touch down safely. Many prayers of thanks were said. Praise the lord!

I recall another thrilling flight, this one, however, on a rare crystal-clear Hump day. As we set down on the runway at Luliang, China, the plane slowed down faster than normal and started pulling to the left. Severe vibrations shook the plane. Cautiously I pushed the right rudder and right brake. The vibrations became so severe we ran off the runway. I applied more right brake and slight left throttle to prevent a ground loop. The plane came to rest 30 feet off the runway, inclining on its left side. My first thought was FIRE. "Get out of here in a hurry!" I yelled. The Luliang emergency crews rushed to our aid, but there was no fire. The good Lord was again watching over us.

What went wrong? Simple—our left tire had gone flat in flight! The flight home to Misamari was beautiful.

Best wishes.
Robert E. Smith

Houston, TX

Dear Dr. Constein,

I was sent to Chungking very early in the war, two and a half years, in fact, before you arrived in Chabua on the India side in the fall of 1944. From the beginning, I enjoyed the adventure. A month after I got there, the crew I flew with picked up General Doolittle and his crew in China after his famous "30 seconds over Tokyo" raid. Before I left the CBI theater of operations, I had flown 75 round-trip flights over the Hump.

I was a Staff Sergeant crew chief at the time of the Burma evacuation in March 1942. The Army Air Corps received several planes but no pilots to fly them. I told my CO, Major Wayne K. Richardson, that I had had a private flying license since I was 16. When he was transferred to Stilwell's headquarters as Air Officer and First pilot, he took me with him as crew chief and acting copilot! I will always remember a certain flight into Kweilin, just a short flight from Japanese air bases.

Flying Vinegar Joe's personal C-47, marked "Japanese Jackass" in Chinese, we landed in the late afternoon. This former Flying Tiger base was home to the 23rd Fighter Group and the 11th Bombardment Squadron of the China Air Task Force. Based there were 31 P-40Bs, and 20 P-40Es.

We parked the plane and headed for the mess hall. Suddenly we noticed a red air raid ball being hoisted on the warning pole. We were not terribly concerned, for only three balls meant an attack was imminent. Besides, it would soon be dark, and the Japanese as a rule did not attack at night. Then a second ball was hoisted. We rushed to the plane, cranked up the engines and pulled Stilwell's baby to the protection of some trees. As we reached the mess hall, we saw two P-40s taking off. We took our chow to a bomb shelter and ate supper without great concern. We were still there when we saw the lights of the two P-40s as they landed. They had been gone about 45 minutes. Word spread around the base that the two P-40s had downed a Zero.

The next morning we returned to Chungking. As I was arranging for a Jeep at the field, a Signal Corps Officer approached and asked what we knew about the raid on Kweilin last night. That seemed awfully mysterious to me. I was struck by his intensity.

My concern was justified. After ten minutes or so he told us what had apparently happened. The officer handled all the messages in and out of Stilwell's headquarters and had been informed by someone at Kweilin that the downed Jap Zero was really one of our own P-40s. The mistaken identity was probably caused by the hazy dusk and by the old AC markings on the P-40, which included a red ball.

After the war I continued on in aviation, serving 30 years as a captain for Delta Airlines. The Kweilin incident of my youth has always stayed in my mind. It had been a hot issue, but nothing ever came of it—no name, no nothing. One of the two P-40 pilots later confided in another pilot. Morale was completely shattered for weeks afterward.

The mystery remains. At one time I ran into a writer from Norton, Massachusetts, who dug into it, but to no avail. It remains an unsolved CBI mystery—at least as far as I am concerned.

I came home with a few medals—a Silver Star and a Bronze Star for the Burma evacuation, two Air Medals and the DFC for flight service, and several campaign ribbons. I also received Chinese Air Force wings.

Sincerely,
Jim Shannon

Lt. Constein, 1945. He says that after 57 years he is still trying to get the monkey off his back.

GLOSSARY

AAC - Army Air Corps, predecessor to the US Air Force

AACS - Army Airways Communication Service

ADF - Automatic Direction Finder, a radio compass which points to the station to which it is tuned

Air Medal - awarded for meritorious achievement in aerial operations

Air Commandos - supplied troops and supplies to Merrill's Marauders and Wingate's Chidits behind enemy lines in Burma

ATC - Air Transport Command, the command that ultimately ran the supply mission of the Hump

Aural Null - To locate a radio beacon with this method, the pilot rotates the antenna until he hears nothing.

Balloon Blowers - good-natured nickname for AAC weathermen

Bamboo Bomber - Cessna AT advanced trainer

Basha - bamboo, thatched-roof barracks for US forces in India and Burma

Below Minimum - Pilots may not land when a field's ceiling and visibility are below minimum standards for that field.

Betty - Japanese twin-engine bomber

Burma Road - 770-mile serpentine road from Lashio, Burma, to Kunming, China. It was built by hand by 100,000 Chinese workers. When it was severed by the Japanese, the Hump airlift took over.

Cargo Kicker - crewman whose job it was to kick cargo out of planes behind enemy lines in Burma,.

CATF - Chinese American Task Force

CAVU - ceiling and visibility unlimited

CBI VA - China-Burma-India Veterans Association

Chicken Colonel - full colonel

CO - Commanding officer

CTD - College Training Detachment. To provide newly-enrolled Aviation Cadets with academic training before they were sent to Pre-flight School, they were housed and given instruction at colleges throughout the country for six to eight weeks.

Combat Cargo - supplied Allied forces, often behind enemy lines

Crab - to turn the plane into a crosswind for the purpose of holding course relative to the ground

CQ - Charge of quarters

Crew Chief - engineer in charge of a plane's maintenance. In the CBI he sometimes flew as a member of the aircrew.

Deadhead - A pilot or crew member who is being transported in the rear of the plane is deadheading.

DFC - Distinguished Flying Cross. Awarded for heroism or outstanding achievement in aerial operations. A step up from the Air Medal.

Ding How - most common greeting in China

Direction Finding - Aircrews uncertain of their plane's position (usually in bad weather) call for a fix. Triangulation units on the ground, if they can be reached by radio, determine the planes position and notify the crew.

DZ - drop zone

EM - enlisted man

ETA - estimated time of arrival, important information on a flight plan

Ferry Command - ATC's Ferry Command delivered new planes as required. Some experienced pilots had that assignment before coming to the CBI.

First Ridge - The first substantial Himalayan ridge (about 7,000 feet high) which Hump crews had to contend with. It required loaded planes heading to China from bases in Assam to climb over an assigned radio beacon until they reached 10,000 feet.

Flying Tigers - American Volunteer Group. P-40 pilots who, before WWII started, for seven months established a remarkable record of shooting down Japanese planes in China

FUO - fever of unknown origin

Gooney Bird - nickname for Douglas C-47 (DC-3)

"Greetings from the President" - Pleasant introduction to unpleasant news—you are drafted!

Holding - In bad weather and heavy air traffic, planes are stacked up over the airfield. The tower orders them to hold at an assigned altitude, to descend to a new assigned altitude (usually 500 feet lower), and finally gives clearance to land.

HPA - Hump Pilots Association

Hubba, Hubba - enthusiastic mock war cry

IFR - Instrument flight rules. Pilot flies and navigates by instruments.

"Kilroy Was Here" The ubiquitous Kilroy left his message for American troops all over the world.

Ledo Road - A road from Ledo, India, to Lashio, Burma, built to connect to the Burma Road.

Link Trainer - an early flight simulation trainer

MAAM - Mid Atlantic Air Museum (of WWII planes) in Reading, PA. Site of a popular early June "WWII Weekend" encampment

Mayday - international distress signal for planes and ships. The Anglicized word is from the French phrase "m'aider" meaning "help me."

MIA - missing in action

Monsoon - an April-to-October wind on the Indian Ocean, blowing from the southwest, bringing heavy and frequent rains, as much 100 inches a month in each of April, May, and June

MOS - military occupational specialty

MP - Military Police

NCO - non-commissioned officer

NYD - not yet diagnosed

OCS - Officer Candidate School, turning out remarkable "ninety-day wonders"

OD - Officer of the day

Ole Dumbo - C-46

One-O-Nine-Boom - popular name for the C-109, a flying gas tank converted from a

Pick's Pike - the Ledo Road. CO of this remarkable engineering feat was Brigadier General Lewis G. Pick. The alliterative name is probably a play on Pike's Peak,

Rock Pile - the highest, most rugged and fearsome area of the Hump

RON - remain over night

R&R - rest leave (literally "rest and relaxation")

Sacred Cow - B-29

St. Elmo's Fire - In cumulonimbus storms, aircrews at times experienced the effects of visible electric discharges off props and within the cockpit. St. Elmo is the patron saint of sailors.

Shoot Landings - to practice landings by landing and immediately taking off

Shore Patrol - Naval MPs assigned to shore duty (SP)

Short Snorter - When a military person crossed the Equator, friends signed his dollar bill, and he signed theirs.

SNAFU - Situation normal: all fouled up

SSO - special services officer

Stilwell Road - another name for the Ledo Road

TDY - temporary duty

Triangulation - Aircrews uncertain of their plane's position called for a radio fix. Triangulation units on the ground determined the plane's position and notified the crew.

Troop Carrier -ferried American and Allied troops wherever needed in the CBI. Sometimes flew supplies.

Valley flights - milk-run flights from Assam west to cities in India

VFR - visual flight rules. Pilot navigates by reference to the ground.

WX - weather .

BIBLIOGRAPHY

Books of likely interest to readers of these letters

Bond, Charles R. Jr. and Anderson, Terry H. *A Flying Tiger's Diary.* Texas A & M Press, 1993

Booby, Robert I. *Food-Bomber Pilot—China-India-Burma* The subtle WWII romance of a CBI pilot with the nurse who saved his life. ISBN 0-9625-5940-7

Boyington, Col. Gregory (Pappy). *Baa Baa Black Sheep*. Putnam, 1977

Chan, Won-loy. *Burma, the Untold Story.* Presidio Press, 1986

Constein, Carl F. *Born to Fly the Hump.* 1st Books Library, 2001

Deetherage, Ben. *Silhouettes of Fear.* Western Printers, 1998. "Through the eyes of one who sits behind the pilot"

Dmitir, Ivan. *Flight to Everywhere.* McGraw Hill, 1954

Downie, Don and Ethell, Jeff. *Flying the Hump. Motorbooks International, 1995*

Genovese, Capt. J. Gen. *We Flew Without Guns.* Winston, 1945

Gordon and staff. *Wings; From Burma to the Himalayas.* Wolf, 1992.

Koenig, William. *Over the Hump: Airlift to China.* Ballantine Books, 1972

Martin, John G. *It Began at Imphal: The Combat Cargo Story.* Sunflower U. *Press, 1988*

Moser, Don. *China-Burma-India (Time Life WWII Books),* 1978

Ogburn, Charlton Jr. *The Marauders.* Harper, 1956

Quinn, Chick Marrs, *The Aluminum Trail.* Sequin Press, 1989

Severeid, Eric. *Not So Wild a Dream.* U of Missouri Press, 1995

Spencer, Otha C. *Flying the Hump.* Texas A & M Press, 1992.

Spencer, Otha C. *Flying the Weather.* The Country Studio, 1996.

Special Service Officer, Hq. Ramgarh Training Center. *Now It Can Be Told.* 1942

Steinbicker, Joseph H. *How Come I'm Still Here?* 1stBooks Library, 2002

Tunner, William H. *Over the Hump.* Duell, Sloan, Pearce, 1964.

White, Edwin Lee. *Ten Thousand Tons by Christmas.* Valkyrie, 1975

White, Theodore H. and Jacoby, Annalee. *Thunder Out of China.* Sloan, 1946.

Withers, Monroe S. *A Texan in the CBI.* Green Valley Press, 1993.

INDEX

ABOUT THE AUTHOR

Carl Frey Constein was born in the eastern Pennsylvania town of Fleetwood. After working his way through college, he became a WWII aviation cadet and received his wings as pilot. He was sent to India to fly supplies and materiel to China over the Himalayan Hump. For his ninety-six round-trip flights he was awarded two Air Medals and the Distinguished Flying Cross. He recalled his year in the China-India-Burma theater in the memoir *Born to Fly the Hump,* published by lstBooks Library.

After the war Constein earned a doctorate at Temple University in English and Educational Administration. He has been a teacher, curriculum director, education writer, and superintendent of schools.

Constein lives outside Reading in Berks County, Pennsylvania. He lectures frequently about the Hump and the CBI to historical societies, aviation groups, library groups, and civic clubs. He is at work on a partly whimsical novel about an author whose books are published by a new breed of publishers.

Printed in the United States
5651